THE
INDISPENSABLE
ELEMENT

Six Keys to Lead Yourself to Success in Your Life, Work, and Relationships

Micah E. Huggins

WELCOME, LEADER!

I commend you for taking a big step toward your personal and professional development.

This book is more than just a memoir or a guide to leadership. It's a roadmap for transformation. I have encountered difficult obstacles throughout my life, such as my father's passing and a traumatic car accident. However, I never allowed these experiences to defeat me.

As an accomplished model, pastor, and top criminal defense attorney in Greensboro, North Carolina, I utilize my personal journey to motivate others to cultivate robust leadership skills rooted in faith. My ultimate goal is to encourage individuals to enhance their lives and make a positive impact within their communities.

I invite you to connect with me beyond this book for more ways to sharpen your leadership skills.

Find me on Instagram: @micah_e_huggins

Get involved in The Model Leader community.

Websites
www.themodelleader.com
www.micahhuggins.com
www.abidinglovechurch.org

Scan the QR code below to access my free resource,
"Are You a Leader or an Imitator?"

This powerful tool will help you uncover whether you are a true leader or an imitator and the steps you need to take to become a leader worth following.

DEDICATION

I dedicate this book to my dear wife, Lauren Michele Huggins, and to our wonderful children, Abigail, Aiden, and Alexander. May you, our children, grandchildren, and many generations to come carry the mantle and legacy of leadership in every area of life.

To my late father, Alonza P. Huggins, and my loving mother, Gladys E. Huggins: thank you for modeling and imparting the principles of leadership and faith.

Lastly, I dedicate this book to every mentor, professor, friend, and counselor who has poured into me in some way, in any season of my life. I appreciate the value you added to my life, character, and ability to lead.

CONTENTS

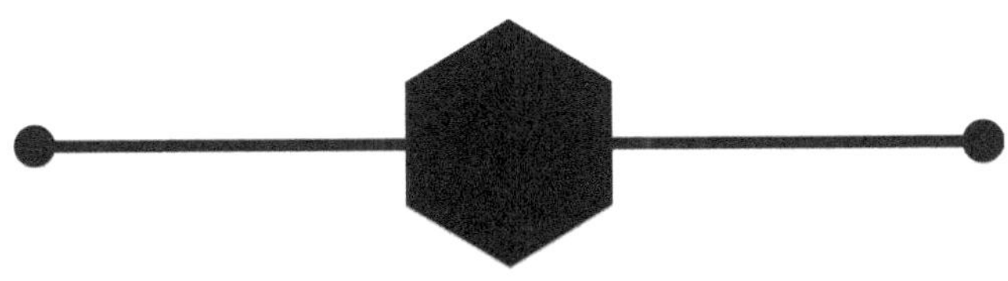

LEAD YOUR WAY TO THE
LIFE YOU WANT

AS MY FATHER drove his truck down the road, I sat in the passenger seat and attempted to school him on what I was learning from the ministers whose work I was studying. As a young man just growing into my own relationship with God, I wanted to get more out of my spiritual life, and for me, that included making changes in my father's church, my church home. I wanted my father to apply what these ministers were doing in the small church he'd founded and pastored. As he sat in silence, I went on and on, dropping knowledge.

Finally, my father snapped. "Boy, if you say one more word to me about that minister! He's not the one there for you, picking you up when you fall. He's not the one praying for you when you're sick. Why do you keep telling me what he says?"

"That man's my spiritual father," I replied. "Don't talk about him like that."

My father hit the brakes, and we skidded to a stop. "Get out of my truck," he said. "If that man's your spiritual father, let him take you home."

We were in the middle of nowhere, at least a fifteen-minute drive from home, on a hot summer day, but I got out of the truck, and I watched as he drove away, leaving me there on the side of the road. I started walking home in the summer heat, and after a short while, a guy I knew stopped to give me a ride. He happened to be someone who'd bullied me when we were kids, but in our twenties, we'd left that history behind us. I poured my heart out to him, and he listened patiently. It was good to talk through it all, but that argument with my father was a turning point for me.

For months, there had been a growing tension between us. As a young man, I was ready to move on from my father's church and seek spiritual experiences and growth elsewhere. Like many parents, my father was reluctant to let me go. In hindsight, I realize he may have seen my desire to seek mentorship from other spiritual leaders as a sign that he was losing me. He may have believed I didn't appreciate the positive impact he'd had on my life up to that point. I may have tapped into some insecurities he had by seeking spiritual guidance elsewhere, and I made the situation worse by going on about what those other ministers were doing. As a Christian, I expected him to be more mature about the situation, but my father was only human. Seeing me spreading my spiritual wings, flying away in search of something more, hit a nerve.

The decision to find a new church home had been brewing for some time, but after that argument in his truck, I finally made it a reality and left my father's church. I thought if this man would leave me out in the middle of the road, then I didn't want him to be my pastor anymore. I was ready to surround myself with people who could take me to the next level in my life. The following Sunday, even though I knew it would hurt my father deeply, I didn't show up for service. I told him I was leaving his church, and I stopped talking to my parents altogether.

This falling-out came at the worst possible time. After three years of hard work and struggle, I'd graduated law school and was trying to pass the bar. My whole life was consumed with studying. Because I didn't have a full-time position yet, I lived with my older brother for a while, but he kicked me out of his house when I couldn't pay rent. Over two months, I studied twelve to fourteen hours a day. I did everything I could to prepare. I spent $600 to take the test. And I failed.

The following months were some of the most difficult of my life. I had to study just as intensely to take the bar again. I felt the pain of the damaged relationship with my parents. I was disappointed that I couldn't rely on my older brother to support me. And my money was short. I had reached a crossroads in my life.

During this time, I prayed and asked God what he wanted me to do. Following his direction, I began to visit other churches, and at one church, I found a leadership with a big vision, something I wanted to be connected to. I joined that church and found what would be my church home for years. I found the support system I needed at that time in my life. I found the mentors I needed for my spiritual growth. I found service that allowed me to develop and mature as a leader. And I met the love of my life, Lauren.

THE ONLY WAY TO GET WHAT YOU WANT

Eventually, my father apologized and told me he loved me, words he rarely said. We repaired our relationship, and until his passing, we were as close as I'd hoped we would be. Today, I have so much of what I wished for back then. I've achieved much of what seemed impossible to me during that dark period of my life. I'm a licensed attorney with a thriving, respected law practice. I've started a church plant, where I minister to a growing faith community. I live in a beautiful, comfortable home with my lovely, smart, and supportive wife, Lauren, and our three amazing kids. I've continued my part-time modeling career and even had the opportunity to do family shoots with my wife and children. As an ethical goal-achievement expert and leadership mentor, I have the fulfillment that comes from helping my clients and audiences grow into their full potential. I've created so much of the life I dreamed of having, and I'm just getting started. Even though I continue to face challenges along the way, I now know what it takes to overcome them. I know what it takes to get what you want out of life.

In my work as a defense attorney and as a pastor, I often counsel people at their lowest. They may face different obstacles than I've encountered, but whatever those obstacles are, there's only one way over them. There's only one way to get to the other side and create the life you want. It doesn't matter how smart you are, how much money you have, or who you know. If you don't have this one indispensable element, it's almost impossible to create the life you dream of living.

Your ability to lead is the indispensable element in creating the life you want. If you have a desire to live a bigger life, you can. You can do work you love every day. You can launch the business you've dreamed of running. You can start a ministry or your own nonprofit organization. You can strengthen your family and raise your children to be productive adults who love the Lord. Whatever dreams you've come close to giving up on, whatever goals you've set for yourself, you can achieve them when you step up as the leader in your own life.

THE TRUTH ABOUT LEADERS

Our culture has misled us about leadership in many ways. Most people believe leadership is reserved for the special few because that's what we're taught. We're constantly told certain people are born leaders, which means by default that everyone else isn't. But the truth is that we're all given gifts that position us to lead in unique ways. It's through this gift-based leadership that we can achieve our most ambitious goals.

As you read *The Indispensable Element*, keep these five important truths about leaders in mind:

1. Leaders *don't* have to know it all.
2. Leaders *don't* have to do it all.
3. Leaders often have to follow.
4. A title *doesn't* make a leader.
5. Leaders are *not* born. They're developed.

Once you recognize, understand, and accept these truths, you'll be better positioned to tap into your own leadership ability. You'll be able to step up, first, as the leader in your own life. You'll identify your God-given gifts and understand how they're meant to help you fulfill your life's purpose. You'll craft a vision for your life, create plans to make that vision your reality, and execute on those plans.

HOW TO USE THIS BOOK

As you read this book, think about the concepts not in some vague way but as each one applies to you and your life. Consider which of these areas are already strengths for you and in which areas you need to improve. You'll retain much more of the information you find here if you take notes as you read. It's also important to take action right away. At the end of each chapter, you'll find my indispensable action steps, some of which follow my ADA formula: assess, decide, act. These steps give you the chance to process and reflect, make a decision, and then put your decision into action. Take the time to work through these exercises in a notebook or journal before you move on to the next chapter. This isn't a race to the finish line. You'll get the most value by doing the work as you read. You can also discuss these action steps with your reading partner or book group.

You can maximize what you'll read here by studying the content and sharing the exercises with other people who are ready to step up as leaders. Consider reading this book chapter by chapter with a study group, book club, or accountability partner. That kind of support can be invaluable and will give you all a chance to benefit from each other's experiences. In addition, the more ways you approach the material—reading, writing, discussing—the easier it will be for you to remember and implement it.

Lastly, stay coachable. Pray for God's guidance and wisdom. And get ready to make decisions and take action to change your life.

FIRST, LEAD YOURSELF

It shall not be so among you. But whoever would be great among you must be your servant, and whoever would be first among you must be your slave, even as the Son of Man came not to be served but to serve, and to give his life as a ransom for many.
Matthew 20:26–28, ESV

EVERY AFTERNOON, WHEN the school bus drove up to our house, I hurried off and hoped the driver pulled away before anyone noticed the shattered windows on our garage. I worried the other kids would realize our house was the shabbiest in the neighborhood and see me as poor. So much about my family's lifestyle embarrassed me back then. Neighbors complained about the all-night barking of the hound dogs my father kept in the yard, and the brand-name clothes other kids wore to school were out of reach for my brother and me. To top it all off, my father was a preacher, and our family was in church a lot, two more things that made us different from most kids I knew. Needless to say, I rarely invited friends over. "If God is so good," I wondered, "why can't we have what everybody else has?"

As a young boy, I dreamed of living in a well-decorated, spacious house I could be proud to invite friends to visit. I wanted to wear brand-name clothes and drive a luxury car when I grew up. When I dreamed about the future, I focused mostly on material things and what the world told me mattered. I didn't realize my parents were giving me something much more important than any possessions. Throughout my childhood, they taught me the values I'd live by for the rest of my life, the same values that helped me develop the ability to achieve any goal I set for myself by becoming the leader in my own life and a leader for the people in the circles I move in.

God *is* good. And in his goodness, he has given you and me everything we need to get whatever we want, usually by helping other people get what they want and need. As my business and my ministry grow, I'm called to serve more people in bigger ways. I trust that I'll continue to prosper because I continue to take the leadership role first in my own life and then in my circles of influence. And I trust God to do the rest.

My story isn't some heroic folktale of pulling myself up by my own bootstraps. I did work hard—I still do. But like anyone who accomplishes big goals, I had help along the way. No one makes it all on their own, and if they say they did, they're either too immature to recognize how many people shared wisdom and opportunities with them or they're lying. Most significantly, I had two amazing leaders in my life who taught me, from an early age, the importance of my relationship with God and of living according to a value system in alignment with the teachings of God's word: my parents. They didn't have all the outward trappings of success, but they taught me how to create any version of success I want in my own life and were my greatest mentors.

LEAD YOUR WAY TO THE LIFE YOU DESIRE

While God has, in fact, given us everything we need—the gifts, the abilities, the ideas, the strategies, and the models and mentors—to create the life we want, most people never quite get there. Most people settle for work that pays the bills instead of using their gifts to do work they love, work that would also position them to achieve the financial freedom they desire. They compromise in their expectations of their relationships and accept mediocrity from themselves and the people around them. When their dreams don't come true right away, most people come to see their goals as unattainable, and they blame other people or the unfairness of life for why they can't do better, be better, or have better. In the end, they give up because they're missing the indispensable element of success—the ability to lead.

Why do so many people fail to achieve the life they want even with so many resources available? They're suffering a kind of poverty money alone can't remedy. They lack the ability to step fully into their role as the leader of their own lives. They shy away from leading others the moment it gets uncomfortable. Most people fall short of their potential because they don't know how to lead their way to greatness. Many don't believe they can.

The truth is you might achieve some of your goals without becoming a leader. It's possible, but you'll never accomplish all you could. Developing as a leader—in every role you fill in your life—is the only way to maximize your potential. The idea that leaders are born, not made, is a fallacy. It's a myth perpetuated by a culture that likes to single out a chosen few as special and capable of changing the world. No one is a born leader. However, we are all, every one of us, born with gifts. In developing and using our gifts to serve others, we grow into leaders.

Leadership is the use of your gifts and talents to create positive influence and increase the value other people contribute to society and humanity for the greater good, while also fulfilling your calling and purpose. Leaders do this by creating space and opportunity for people to develop their gifts. No one is a born leader because you can't call yourself a leader until you're wielding your influence and using your gifts for the greater good. This level of leadership requires you to live by a set of values that keeps you focused on the right things. As you read further, you'll find you already apply some of the principles outlined here. Becoming aware of them will allow you to fine-tune your practice of these principles and address some you may have ignored as you grow and develop as a leader.

You are called to leadership. You may lead at the helm of an international corporation or on the front lines of a small business. You may lead as a parent, a sibling, or a friend, but leadership is your birthright and your responsibility. No matter who you are or what you do for a living, you have opportunities to lead every day. However, before you take the lead in any effective way in those areas of your life, you must first lead yourself. Recognizing and stepping up to your calling to lead yourself and others is the single act that will position you to have the life you dream of living. It may sound like a huge task, but you were made for this.

We're all called to lead in some capacity, but most people go through life largely unaware of their leadership potential. Most simply answer that calling unconsciously, wherever it comes easiest and most naturally to them, never fully developing their leadership skills. They step up on occasion in different areas of life but never fully claim their place as a leader. Others abuse their ability to lead. They use their influence to encourage people down the wrong path for their own selfish reasons. Whatever they produce is built on a foundation of manipulation and greed, and it cannot last.

Then, there are the few who get intentional about developing themselves as leaders. They use their influence to fulfill their purpose and complete their life's mission. These people understand the power and responsibility of leadership and take their role seriously as they work to serve others and accomplish their own goals. These leaders effect positive change in our world. They help the people around them develop their own gifts, and they enjoy the rewards of that contribution. They're the great leaders of nations but also the great leaders of small businesses, households, classrooms, and firehouses.

They're people just like you, who decide every day to exercise their leadership ability for the good of everyone in their circles of influence.

It's important to keep in mind that influence and leadership aren't the same thing. While leadership, the way I define it, is always for a greater good, influence can be used for good or evil. Martin Luther King Jr. led a movement that propelled this country closer to equality for all people, opening doors that had been closed for centuries, by taking action that led to the passing of the Civil Rights Act of 1964. At the other end of the spectrum of influence, an estimated three hundred thousand people were murdered under brutal Ugandan dictator Idi Amin's influence. Both men wielded the weight of their authority, one for the betterment of his people and his country and the other to feed his own lust for power while devastating a nation. Both achieved many of their goals. But only one was a leader.

Successful rappers have influence over millions of their fans. Yet, many of them choose to abuse this influence. They casually toss around foul language, and they glorify drug use and alcohol abuse. These men—and increasingly, women—refer to women as "bitches" and "hoes." They normalize the idea of having multiple sex partners and having children with multiple "baby mamas" and "baby daddies." They encourage the hyper-sexualization of girls and women and treat their own bodies as anything but sacred. They throw around words like "nigga" with no thought to the consequences.

These influencers contribute to the degradation of women and the decline of our society. They influence their followers to focus on self-glorification. While many people look up to them, follow them, and even want to be like them, they're not leaders. You cannot use your gifts exclusively for your own benefit and to the detriment of other people and call yourself a leader. When you choose to use your gifts to destroy rather than create, you betray the consecrated value of leadership for selfish gain.

This is just one example of the misuse of influence that's so common in today's society. We could find many more across industries, from entertainment to education, from the Church to charitable organizations, from your local market to the stock market. No arena is exempt from self-centered influence. As you read this book, keep in mind that these people are *not* leaders. We cannot afford to bestow the title of "leader" on everyone so freely. The information presented here is predicated on the idea that you desire to become not just an influencer or a powerful person but a *true leader.*

Leaders strive to reach personal goals but always look to serve as positive role models for the people they influence. They're willing to sacrifice short-term desires to achieve long-term objectives. They take their followers along with them on their journey to the mountaintop. They use their influence for the greater good and employ their gifts while helping others develop their own gifts.

In recent years, "influencer" has become a pseudo job title with sponsorships, brand deals, and constant attention and adoration attached to it, so let's get clear about the meaning of the word. An influencer is simply a person who can convince other people to change their beliefs and behaviors—for better or worse. Every leader is an influencer, but not every influencer is a leader in the way we're using the word here. You can become an influencer without ever giving a thought to the well-being of your fans and followers or how your influence affects them. As an influencer, you can choose to make decisions based solely on what's best for you. As a leader, however, any pursuit of your own goals takes into consideration how other people will also be affected and will benefit from your achievements.

A leader influences people to walk in their own purpose while also persuading them to help the leader achieve his or her goals and serve a greater good. A leader draws on the gifts of his or her followers while pouring into those followers and helping them develop their gifts and their own leadership skills. A true leader is selfless, daring, and willing to take calculated risks. Leadership requires you to become self-aware, recognizing your gifts and your strengths and weaknesses. It demands hard work and perseverance because leaders don't quit even when the odds seem stacked against them. They change their lives and the world for the better by finding a way to keep going.

CIRCLES OF INFLUENCE

The goals you set for yourself, the life you want to create, the wealth you want to build, and the relationships you want to nurture all require you to lead in some way in your circles of influence. Every one of us has circles of influence in which we can have an impact. When you choose to develop as a leader and have an intentional positive impact in these areas, you can create the life you desire with the kind of relationships, accomplishments, and results few people get to enjoy.

YOUR CIRCLES OF INFLUENCE, IN WHICH YOU CAN
DEMONSTRATE LEADERSHIP, INCLUDE THE FOLLOWING:

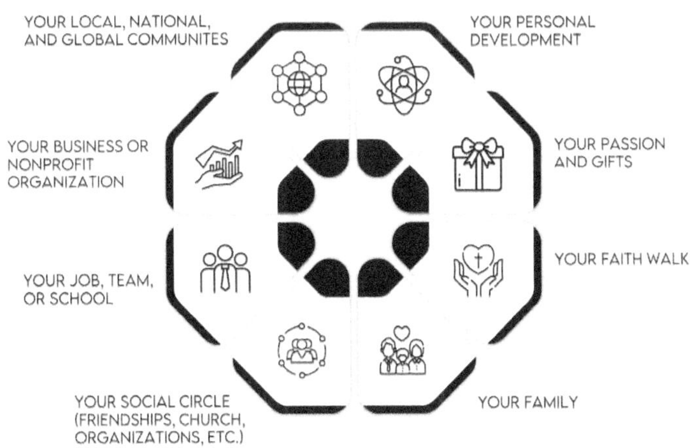

At the center of your circles of influence is you. This is where leadership starts. Your ability to lead others and influence their lives is determined by your willingness and ability to lead in your own life. Your willingness to take the lead in your personal development, in growing your gifts and pursuing your passion, and in your faith walk will determine how much you influence those outer circles. Your family, the people you work with, go to school or church with, or spend your leisure time with, your friends and acquaintances, and your larger community—as you develop as a leader, you'll find yourself naturally exerting greater influence in those circles. You'll not only transform your own life, but your growth will have a ripple effect that reaches further than you can imagine.

OBSTACLES TO LEADERSHIP

Years ago, I met a master chef who worked for a major hotel chain and had been the leading chef there for a decade. He had a reputation as the best chef in the organization, and his skills backed that up. For years, he talked about starting his own company, but never took action to make it happen. In 2020, however, the COVID-19 pandemic finally pushed him out of his comfort zone when stay-at-home orders and lockdowns hit the hospitality industry hard. Only then did he put his trust in his gifts, skills, and experience and take the leap to build a business of his own.

If you asked him, this chef might say he launched his business at that time because the timing was finally right. But from my perspective, everything he did during the pandemic he could have done years earlier. He had the wisdom and experience. He just needed to step out on faith and act.

There are times when you need to mature in your gifts or your character before you can rise to the next level of leadership in your work, your relationships, your community, or your walk with God.

However, once you achieve that maturity, you still have to take action. You have to do something. That action always involves risk, and risk-taking requires faith. You can't wait to know everything and cover every angle before you take a risk and step up as a leader. The time when you've eliminated any chance of failure will never come.

Too often people run into one of the obstacles to leadership and allow it to delay or deny them. This is completely unnecessary because there's always a way to get over these obstacles. You can overcome any external obstacle—a lack of cash, a lack of support, or a lack of information—when you've developed your leadership skills, and you can recover from any setback if you deal with your internal obstacles first. Most of those internal obstacles fall into one of three categories: (1) fear, (2) a lack of confidence, or (3) entitlement.

Fear stops most people from ever stepping fully into leadership. They're afraid of being rejected if they try something different from what everyone else in their circle is doing. They don't want to pursue a big goal because they're afraid of feeling like a failure—and being seen as a failure—if it doesn't work out the way they planned. They never take a chance on themselves because they're waiting for the perfect moment or some kind of guarantee, but there is no perfect moment, and the guarantee isn't coming. So, they let fear keep them from achieving greatness in their lives, and they cheat the world out of what they have to offer.

Similar to fear, a lack of confidence is a major obstacle to leadership. A lack of self-confidence stops many people from going all in as leaders. They don't trust themselves to know enough or to learn what they need to know. They don't believe they can be better today than they were yesterday. Others lack faith, not in themselves but in God's promises. When it comes down to it, they don't believe God has their back, so they try to take their destiny into their own hands. They resist partnering with God's power to fulfill their purpose. They try to lead from their own strength, which will never be sufficient in and of itself. This lack of faith in oneself or in God is a huge obstacle to leadership, but like fear, it can be overcome.

Finally, many people are stopped from becoming the exceptional leaders they could be by their sense of entitlement. They believe it should all come easily to them. They want to ride on their talents without putting in the time and effort to nurture the gifts God gave them. They're not willing to be patient in the face of setbacks. They want overnight success, and they believe they deserve it. Fortunately, this sense of entitlement, like all these internal obstacles, can be overcome with the Six Keys to Leadership.

LEADERS FAIL TOO

There's no escaping the fact that you have weaknesses that can hinder your ability to lead. We all do. Every leader has flaws. Those people who led nations, fought for the underdog, or created massive enterprises that employed thousands of people and produced products that benefited society all had flaws. Some had dark secrets only revealed long after they were out of power or after their deaths. For others, those secrets brought their leadership to an untimely end, but the greatest leaders recognized their flaws and made overcoming them a part of their life's work.

To develop your strength as a leader, examine your weaknesses in two areas: (1) your craft and (2) your character. Craft weaknesses are simple to address. You can easily assess your performance in your craft and identify any shortcomings you must address or have a wise mentor give you feedback. You may need practice, study, or coaching. You may need to partner with someone who can offset your weakness with their strength. There's always a solution to resolve or supplement a weakness in your craft.

Once you develop a skill in your craft, you have that new skill. It's yours. You own it. Character flaws, on the other hand, require a different kind of effort. When you recognize a character flaw in yourself, acknowledge that it exists. You're human, and we all fall short, but scripture says God's strength is made perfect in our weakness (2 Corinthians 12:9, KJV). Developing your strength of character will position you for leadership in a way that focusing solely on your skill set won't. Your specific skills won't always be transferable from one role to another, but your character will determine what kind of leader you'll be in any situation.

A character flaw is any behavior you repeatedly exhibit that falls outside the values God has given us to live by. As Christians, we set our values based on the Word of God and the life and teachings of Jesus. Of course, these are very high standards. You're going to fall short sometimes. We all do. While you can never achieve perfection, we must try. Failing to strive to live by these values results in operating in a mode of selfishness, which inevitably hurts you and the people around you.

This is why we all have a conscience—even if we sometimes choose to ignore it for the sake of doing what we want to do. Your conscience doesn't just serve to make you feel guilty when you do something wrong. It's also there to help you grow into the person—the true leader—you were created to be. As you develop the Six Keys to Leadership, you'll become more aware of your value system and how you measure up against it. The guidance in this book will help you get clear about the areas you need to focus on to limit the personal shortfalls that could otherwise prevent you from reaching your maximum potential as a leader.

SIX KEYS TO LEADERSHIP

As a high school student, I made good grades here and there, but I often got distracted. The same pattern repeated over and over. I'd start off doing great, and as the school year went along, I'd lose focus and my grades would slip. Early in my senior year, the guidance counselor called me into her office. She wanted to introduce me to some alternatives to attending college. I had demonstrated my academic potential, but rather than encourage me and help me figure out how to consistently do well, she did her best to discourage me from continuing my education.

My high school counselor didn't think I could make it as a college student. She didn't think I had the discipline to do college-level work, and she saw no reason I should try. Fortunately, her attempts to persuade me to give up on higher education had the opposite effect. Not only did her lack of confidence in me motivate me, so did the endgame. I knew a college degree would open doors that would otherwise remain closed to me forever. Although I was still developing as a leader in my youth, at that decision point, I decided to take the harder road.

Maybe it was a rebellious streak in me, a desire to prove her wrong, but after that conversation, I buckled down. I managed to finish the year with a 3.0 grade point average (GPA), and I went on to enroll at the University of North Carolina at Greensboro. I'd love to tell you I was a star college student from day one; however, that wasn't the case. In my freshman year, I worked hard but I also partied with my friends in the early weeks, until I decided to give my life to Christ. In my sophomore year, I landed my first modeling contract with the agency that still represents me today, and I got distracted by those opportunities, which made me think maybe I didn't need to work so hard. Maybe, I thought, modeling would take me in a different direction.

I was also struggling with undiagnosed attention deficit hyperactivity disorder (ADHD). Just like in high school, every semester, I'd start off strong and then lose interest. One day in my junior year, I was working on a communications studies paper, and I finally got it. Something clicked, and I understood what my professors were looking for in college-level work. That day changed my academic career. I got an A on that paper, and from that day forward, I earned an A on every assignment. During my senior year, by which time I knew I wanted to go to law school, I made nothing less than an A-.

When I decided to apply to law school, six months after getting my undergraduate degree, I looked at both the University of North Carolina at Chapel Hill, the nation's first public university, and North Carolina Central University, a highly ranked historically Black university. Before I made my choice, my father and I went to speak with a dean at Central about their law school. The dean brought us into his office and explained that Central gave its students plenty of support along the way. I looked over at my dad, and he had tears in his eyes as he listened to the dean. Then the dean said, "You can go over there with those White folks if you want, but if you don't make it, you can't come back here. This isn't a dumping ground." And that's when I made up my mind.

His words shocked and challenged me. I couldn't believe a school leader would say something so discouraging in a professional context. I suppose he was taking a "keeping it real" approach, but it wasn't the time or place for that kind of conversation. As a leader, he should have chosen his words more carefully. From my perspective, he should've been making the pitch for why I should attend his school, not making threats. His comments motivated me because it seemed he believed I couldn't make it at Chapel Hill. He had a defeatist mentality, and I didn't like it. I didn't want to start law school expecting the worst.

On the drive home, my dad told me, "I'm pro-Black. I want you to go to Central." I didn't say much in response, but a couple of days later, I reminded my dad what the dean had said about not coming back to Central as a safety net if the program at Chapel Hill proved too tough. "He doesn't think you can do it," my dad said. The dean had lost both of us. I chose to attend Chapel Hill.

When the dean at Central expressed his doubt about my ability to complete the program at Chapel Hill, I decided to prove him wrong. I respected the dean and I loved my dad, but I looked to my left and saw a smooth road and looked to my right and saw a steep mountain with a greater reward at the summit, and I decided to climb the mountain. The journey was filled with treacherous obstacles. As expected, Black students were in the minority at the law school, which was isolating enough; however, striving to live out my Christian values isolated me even more. The law school offered a three-day prep program for underrepresented students, but I didn't find the kind of support I needed on an ongoing basis. Frankly, I struggled through all three years.

At the same time, the words of the Central dean haunted me. In my darkest moments, I wondered if he'd been right, but in those moments, I relied on my faith in God, my determination, and my sense of pride to see me through. I developed my self-confidence and continued to strive for excellence in every class. I usually wasn't the smartest person in the room, but I was smart enough, and I committed to giving 100 percent in every class. I wanted to be a part of the legacy of successful people who had come through that school, and in the end, I took my place among them because I lived by the values great leaders honor.

When Martin Luther King Jr.'s advisors counseled him not to speak out against the Vietnam War, he followed his conscience and spoke for the cause of peace anyway. He took the hard road. He climbed the steep mountain because he was led by his own convictions rather than popular opinions. He was self-governed according to his values, and even though he paid a price, he stepped up as a leader and did what he believed to be right for himself, his people, our country, and the world. Leadership will often require you to take the harder path to get the rewards you desire. Doing so requires a commitment to the values of great leadership.

When Nelson Mandela became president of South Africa after serving twenty-seven years of his life in prison, he could have sought revenge. He could have focused on punishing the unjust leaders who upheld the laws of apartheid for half a century. Instead, he used his position of power to seek reconciliation and move his country in the direction of healing. During his time in prison, he had developed and refined his leadership skills, and he emerged as a world leader. His commitment extended to something much larger than his own needs and desires, making him not just a famous leader or a successful leader but also a great leader.

When Congresswoman Shirley Chisholm sought the Democratic Party's nomination for president in 1972, she had to campaign against five White men also running for the nomination. Ms. Chisholm was already the first Black woman elected to the United States Congress. Thirty-seven years before President Barack Obama took office, she was both the first woman and the first Black person to actively seek nomination as the presidential candidate for a major party. She took her run seriously, and although she failed to secure the nomination, she continued her fight on behalf of social justice issues and education reform in Congress for another decade. She didn't give in to bitterness or regret. As a great leader, she balanced her personal ambition with an unstoppable will to serve the people she represented.

These leaders are famous politicians and activists, but great leadership can be found in corporate boardrooms, classrooms, and around the family dinner table. Great leaders show up in church, and small businesses, and community organizations. They're the fathers who say no to a night out with their friends so they can go to their children's basketball games and dance recitals. They're the mothers who run small businesses that keep dollars in their community while making sure their children get the best possible education. They're the entrepreneurs who create a significant income for themselves while treating their employees with dignity and respect. Consciously or unconsciously, these leaders rely on a common set of values that allow them to achieve their goals while making life better for the people in their circles of influence.

Your ability to lead with greatness in your own life and in your circles of influence is directly tied to the values you choose to use as your life compass. You don't have to be the best student, the smartest person in the room, or the person everyone thinks of as a natural-born leader. You simply need to commit to striving for mastery in the Six Keys of Leadership—a mastery that can never be fully achieved but the pursuit of which will always propel you toward greatness and success in every aspect of your life.

THESE SIX KEYS OF LEADERSHIP ARE ESSENTIAL TO FULFILLING YOUR POTENTIAL AND CREATING THE LIFE YOU DESIRE:

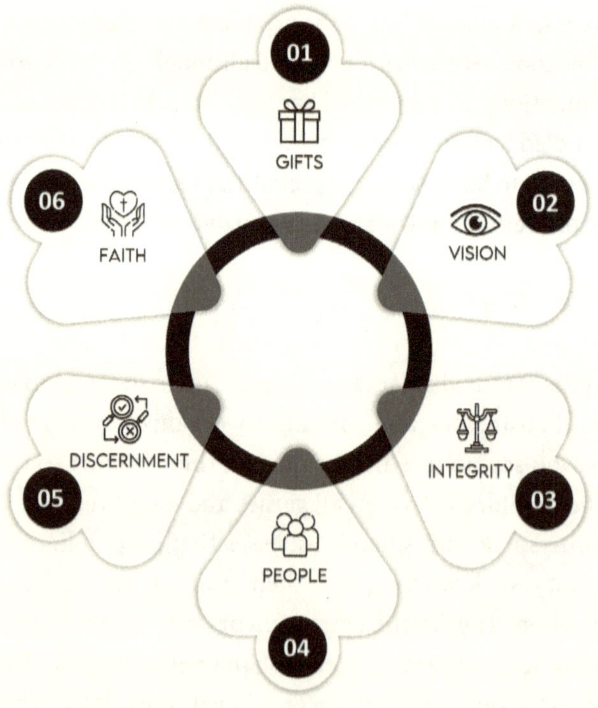

The fact that you're reading a book on leadership tells me you want an extraordinary life. You may want to take control of your career, launch a new business, or start a nonprofit organization that flourishes and changes the world. Perhaps you want to finally walk in your purpose and get clear about your calling. Maybe you want to be more confident and choose your own path without concern for other people's opinions. Whatever change you want to create in your life and in your community, the Six Keys to Leadership are essential to making that change a reality.

Great leaders pay a price to become great. Even if you never have an official leadership role in an organization, that price is still worth paying because developing the qualities of a leader will transform your life and position you to contribute at a higher level. Everybody can't be the captain of the team, but a good second can be just as effective and as important to the success of the team as any captain. A good second can still lead. Even if you're in the lowest position at your place of employment right now, leading yourself to do the best you can in that role influences others. It has a desirable impact. You don't have to be the owner, the manager, or the shift leader for people to see your hustle and your commitment and be inspired. Lead from where you are until you get to where you want to be.

Invest as much in developing your character as you do in pursuing your more tangible goals. That's leadership. That's the indispensable element in creating and maintaining your success.

INDISPENSABLE ACTION STEPS
FIRST LEAD YOURSELF

In a notebook or journal set aside for your leadership development, answer the following questions/complete the following exercises.

Assess.

Do you consider yourself a leader? Why or why not?

Decide.

If you don't yet consider yourself a leader, what do you believe you need to learn to become the leader you aspire to be?

Why do you want to become a great leader? What positive impact do you want to have in your life and the lives of other people?

Write your personal definition of each of the Six Keys to Leadership (gifts, vision, integrity, people, discernment, and faith).

Act.

As you go through the following chapters, be aware of how your perception of the Six Keys to Leadership expands or changes.

GIFTS

Do nothing from selfish ambition or conceit, but in humility count others more significant than yourselves. Let each of you look not only to his own interests, but also to the interests of others.
Philippians 2:3–4, ESV

ALTHOUGH I STARTED telling people I wanted to be an attorney from an early age, I didn't have a clue how that goal aligned with my gifts until I was a senior in high school and decided to take a speech and debate class. The class taught me to create an argument and present it, and I had the opportunity to put those skills to the test on a competitive level. I studied day and night to try to excel at Lincoln–Douglas debating. I worked hard, and while most of the team signed up for the minimum number of debates they could get away with, one friend and I signed up for every debate available to us.

Even though I had to work at it, debate felt natural to me. I had found my niche, but even with all the effort I put into it, I wasn't the best out there. I was a rookie, and some of the students we competed against had been debating for years. They had private coaches. Their schools had a legacy in the field and recruited the best students and coaches for their teams. The competition was tough, but I still loved it. I studied the best speakers and debaters and learned from what they did. I invested most of my free time in improving my skills, including creating and presenting an argument, researching, listening, and communicating clearly and persuasively. Over weeks, my skills improved, and I started winning competitions. At the end of the season, I even won an award at the state level.

I still use those gifts and the skills I developed back then almost every day. As an attorney, I argue on behalf of my clients. As a preacher, I use the text to make an argument for Christ every week. When I met my wife, I had to convince her that I was a man worth getting to know. As a father, I'll have to persuade my children to do what I think is best as they grow older. My gift for speaking has paid off and continues to serve me in many areas of my personal and professional life.

Many people overlook their gifts because they operate in them with such ease, but just as speaking and persuasion came naturally to me, God has given you a unique set of gifts. If you aren't sure what your gifts are, you may be taking them for granted. Whether you realize it yet or not, what comes easily to you is a challenge for many other people. You might be a gifted singer or pianist, a gifted painter or actor. You might be gifted at math, memorizing dates and facts, cooking, or writing poetry. You might be a gifted caregiver or teacher. You could have a gift for encouragement, analytical thinking, or storytelling. The fact is that everyone has gifts, and to maximize your potential and create the kind of success you want in your life, you must tap into those gifts.

RECOGNIZE YOUR GIFTS

The capacity to recognize your gifts and use them to achieve your goals separates leaders from everyone else. Leaders understand they can be passionate about a lot of things, but their passion isn't always the same as their gift. When their passions and gifts don't align, leaders have the wisdom to put passions in their place. In that case, they treat passions as hobbies or side interests and focus most of their time and attention on developing their gifts.

You probably know a young man who's passionate about basketball, but that doesn't mean he's naturally gifted at the sport or destined to play in the NBA. He may enjoy watching games and shooting hoops with his friends. He may even excel on his high school team, but the odds are he can't compete with the best in the world. Sometimes, a passion is meant to be a hobby or serve as entertainment or a path to develop other gifts and skills.

While you shouldn't commit your life to a passion that isn't your gift, you can still learn from it. That same young man who loves basketball, for instance, can learn from the work ethic, dedication, and mental toughness of his favorite basketball players. He can use his time on the high school basketball team to develop those traits in himself. However, he should invest at least as much time in uncovering and developing his God-given gifts as he does in pursuing his passion. While it's fine and even admirable to work on developing any skill, it doesn't make sense to forsake your gift so you can dedicate your life to something you'll never be great at doing.

Never waste time coveting a gift you weren't given. If you weren't gifted with a beautiful singing voice, you can still learn to sing on key. Maybe you can sing in the church choir or sing along with the radio in your car for your own enjoyment, but you're probably not called to be a professional singer. If you were, God would have given you that gift. Don't allow your true gifts to wither on the vine while you run after a purpose that was never meant for you. You won't find your calling by trying to copy someone else's gift.

If you're not sure what your gifts are, don't give up on uncovering them. In fact, it shouldn't be a difficult assignment. Think back to what you were naturally good at as a child. Sometimes, those traits were rewarded, and sometimes, they were overlooked or even punished because the adults around you didn't see their value. That doesn't change the fact that they were gifts given to you by God. The kindergartner who can't sit still might be a gifted gymnast or dancer. The teenager who only wants to talk about their favorite band might be a gifted music producer or concert promoter. The gift isn't good or bad. How you use it will determine its value.

If you need help identifying your gifts, ask the people who knew you when you were growing up what came easily to you. Ask the people who know you best now what they think you're naturally good at. Be open to hearing what other people have to say, but listen to your own voice too. Intuitively, you know what comes easiest to you. As you recognize your gifts, do the work to grow in those areas so you can use your gifts at the highest level to pursue your purpose and answer your calling.

KNOW WHO YOU ARE

When I graduated from high school, like many young adults, I was excited to leave my parents and the rules and regulations that governed life in their house. I thought of them as strict parents, and I couldn't wait to have the freedom to do exactly the opposite of what they'd taught me for eighteen years. Away at college, I could drink as much as I wanted and be with as many women as I wanted, and no one would stop me. In fact, I used my gift for persuasion to talk women into coming home with me. I shared an apartment with my best friend, and we participated in much of the same lifestyle.

During this time, my grades were decent, but I wasn't focused on school. Pretty quickly, I realized I wasn't happy living that way.

School had started in August, and by October, my conscience was telling me I was better than the way I was living. One morning, I woke up and there was a girl lying in bed beside me. "I know better," I thought. I reflected on everything my parents had taught me. I thought about how much money they were paying for my education, and I knew something had to change.

My behavior was a clear indication that I lacked my own identity. I was doing what I saw everyone else do. I was following, not leading, in my own life, so I decided to choose a different path. I wanted to live the way my parents had raised me to, treating women with respect and honoring my body and myself. I stopped following what everyone else was doing and stepped up to lead in my own life. The Holy Spirit began to really deal with me, and I gave my life to Christ.

As I set about changing my lifestyle, I explained to my roommate that I'd given my life to the Lord. "You're going to see a lot of changes in me," I told him. He may not have taken me seriously in the moment, but I made those changes. I emptied my refrigerator of all the stuff that shouldn't have been in there. I stopped bringing women over to the apartment. I replaced the rap music I listened to much of the time with listening to the Word on CDs.

As my roommate realized I really was done with my old ways, he and I grew apart, but for me, there was no turning back. Rather than continue living with him and put up with his friends, who were still participating in everything I was leaving behind, I moved out. I still paid my share of the rent so my roommate wouldn't be left hanging, but I moved back in with my parents. It was one of the best decisions I ever made. My parents were able to mentor me in a new way. I was no longer a child going along with what they said because I had to do it. I was a young man who had willingly stepped up to lead my own life. I was open to learning how to do better, and they were there to teach me.

Jesus came to seek that which is lost, and I'd recognized how lost I was. The way I lived when I first got to college was out of alignment with what the Word of God says about who I am and who we are. The Bible says, over and over, that you are victorious in Christ. It says you have a Heavenly Father and you're a king's kid. When you understand you've been adopted into a royal family, you know who you really are, and you choose to live accordingly. That includes using your gifts to fulfill God's purpose for you.

The only way to know what God says about you is to read the Bible, the mind of God. God won't necessarily speak to you and tell you, "This is who you are to me." You can't wait for him to come inside your house and sit down and teach you about your identity in him. Instead, you have to seek to understand the Word of God. If you struggle to read the Bible, get a more contemporary version, like the *New Living Translation*, the *New International Version*, the *Amplified Bible*, or *The Message*. Download a Bible app with a Bible study plan and read the easy translations. Find a mentor or coach who can provide an understanding of what you're trying to learn and can put you on a path of understanding. Do the work to understand who God says you are so you can begin to use your gifts the way he designed you to use them.

KNOW YOUR TRUE PURPOSE

Your identity as a child of God is inextricably linked to your true and ultimate purpose. Once you know your identity, you'll no longer allow others to define you. You'll no longer have to feel insecure or regret the way you've lived your life. You'll stop following and start leading by living in alignment with what God's word says about you. When you know your true purpose and live accordingly, you can create a life you're proud of by maximizing what you were created to do.

To get clarity about your purpose, answer these three questions:

1. Who am I?
2. Why am I here?
3. What does it matter?

Here are my answers to those questions:

1. Who am I? *I'm a man created by God.*
2. Why am I here? *I'm here to fulfill God's purpose and call upon my life by using the gifts God gave me.*
3. Why does it matter? *When I use my God-given gifts, I give God glory, serve other people, and enjoy the satisfaction and contentment of knowing I've done what I was put here on earth to do.*

Your purpose is to maximize your life, give glory to God in all you do, and become more Christlike in the process. But know this: Purpose isn't a destination; it's a journey. To fulfill your purpose, you'll spend a lifetime using your gifts in service of other people and for the glory of God. Purpose is a way of life.

You're walking in your true purpose when:

1. You use your gift to glorify God.
2. You use your gifts to serve others.
3. You use your gifts to become more like Christ.

The way you use your gifts should always bring glory to God. This can sound like a heavy burden to bear until you understand what it looks like in real life. It simply means you use your gifts to serve humanity—your family, your coworkers, your employees, your employer, your community, your country, and the world—and allow the fulfillment of your purpose to make you more Christlike. When you do this, you bring glory to God. Your own success naturally follows, and the quality of your life improves in the process.

Like influence, any gift can be used for good or evil. Some people use their gift to serve their own ends and hurt people in the process. God didn't make me a charismatic person so I could brag about being the most charismatic person in the room or manipulate people. That gift is meant to draw people to me so I can lead them to God. Con men use the same gift of charisma to win the confidence of their victims. Cult leaders use charisma to convince followers to substitute the leaders' judgment for their own. Crooked politicians use charisma to manipulate people into overlooking their corruption. It's up to you to choose to use your gift for good and fulfill your purpose of glorifying God.

Think of the dancer who spends a lifetime sacrificing, training, and developing her skills, nurturing the gift God gave her. On the night of her big solo performance, she brings joy and comfort to hundreds of people, and as she takes her last bow, palms pressed together, she looks up and gives thanks to God. "All glory for what you just saw me do," she has said without speaking, "belongs to my Father." The chef who prepares every meal with care, the janitor who's done with his shift but notices a blown lightbulb and stays a little later to change it, the teacher who reaches into her own pocket to make sure her students have pencils and paper, the business owner who ensures his employees make a living wage—all these people are on the right path of using their gifts to serve others and allowing those gifts to make them more like Christ.

Understand that you will have to work to develop your gift, but this work is essential to leading with greatness. Just because something comes naturally to you doesn't mean you don't have to invest in it. You can't just coast on your talent. Many gifted people get outworked by people whose gift may not be as great but who are willing to put in the hours to develop it. I'm not the most gifted attorney or even the smartest attorney; however, I work hard to even the playing field so I can be on the same level with the best and use my gifts effectively.

Your gifts are always worth investing in because, used properly, they allow God's love and light to shine through you. God created Jesus to fulfill the purpose of dying on the cross. Jesus brought God glory by fulfilling his purpose of dying for our sins in obedience to God the Father. When you use your gifts and operate in obedience to God's word, you inevitably glorify him and become more Christlike in the process.

Fulfilling your purpose doesn't require you to die on the cross, but you will have to sacrifice. You'll have to be obedient to God and invest time and money to develop and use the gifts he placed in you when he created you. If you're not yet using your gifts to serve people in some way, you are out of God's purpose for you. If you're focused exclusively on what your gifts can do for you, stop and reassess. You can change that today. Allow God's light to shine through you as you use your gifts, and you'll fulfill your true purpose even as you create the kind of life you want and achieve the success you dream of having.

IDENTIFY YOUR CALLING

Your calling is your destiny. It's the work or vocation God is calling you to do. It's that which you are ordained and gifted to do as only you can. Everybody is called to help people—that's part of the definition of our purpose—but we all do it in different ways. To identify your calling, start by looking at your gift. My wife, for example, is a gifted caregiver. Lauren's called to help people by teaching them about healthy childbirth and in her role as a nurse.

I have the gifts of speech and persuasion. I'm called to preach the gospel and leverage the legal system for the benefit of humankind.

When I was in fifth grade, the teacher asked the class what we wanted to be when we grew up. My hand shot into the air, and I told my class I planned to be a lawyer. At the time, I had no idea where that came from, but from that day, I had it in my mind that I wanted to practice the law. In high school, my positive experience with speech and debate confirmed I was on the right path. In college, I majored in political science and communications, and I became fascinated with the law in a more serious way.

I wanted to become an attorney so badly that I'd sit in courtrooms, study the attorneys, and take notes on the different strategies and tactics they used. I read Johnnie Cochran's first book, *Journey to Justice*, and later, I would read *A Lawyer's Life*, the book he published after the trial that made him a household name, the People of the State of California v. Orenthal James Simpson. I was committed, but my journey to becoming an attorney wasn't always easy. In fact, once I started to pursue my law degree, much of the process was an uphill battle, but I was using my gifts, answering my calling, and making progress. Eventually, I made it across the finish line to become a lawyer and build a successful practice of my own.

Becoming a minister of the gospel, on the other hand, was a calling I had to grow into. I always knew I was called to be different; however, I didn't know it would mean preaching God's word. My dad was a pastor, and he started a church when I was a teenager. At that time, I would never have believed I'd one day do the same thing. Occasionally, a man or woman would walk up to me and say something like, "I don't know who you are, but you have a calling on your life," but I didn't yet know what that meant for me.

Although I grew up in church, it wasn't until my freshman year of college that I received my first calling to become a true and authentic Christian and strive to be more like Christ. I wasn't yet called to be a preacher, but I was called to live the life of a believer. In the following years, God used different experiences to prepare me to become a pastor even before I heard him call me to the vocation.

A pastoral role calls for development by God. If that's a calling on your life, you must willingly submit to being developed by God because he has to first prepare the shepherd before the shepherd can lead the sheep. Even when he trusts you enough to start a church and lead his people, God is constantly working on you to build and strengthen your character. Too often, we hear scandalous stories of pastors who end up going rogue. They veer from the life God has called them to lead because they don't remain committed to the developmental process.

Becoming a pastor may not be a part of your calling, but using your gifts, fulfilling your purpose, and answering your calling at the highest level will still require you to submit to God's will. You'll have to be the leader in your own life, and as you grow in your calling, you'll inevitably find yourself in the position to lead other people. You're always in a position to influence and mentor. Creating any amount of success in your life as you answer your calling positions you as a leader. As such, you must be willing to submit to God, just as a pastor must, because any position of leadership can be corrupted. To stay on the path God has for you, ask God to develop your character, knowing you'll serve as an example for those who follow you.

To use your gifts and fulfill your purpose, you must be a good steward of your character. A leader takes responsibility beyond himself or herself. Leaders recognize their ability to influence. Somebody is always watching you, so whether you choose to be or not, for better or for worse, you will be a role model in the way you exercise your gifts. Whatever your calling turns out to be, you're also called to leadership in that arena and in other areas of your life.

ANSWER YOUR CALLING THROUGH YOUR GIFTS

Even as you begin to recognize your gifts, know who you are, and understand your purpose, your calling isn't always obvious. You have to use wisdom and discernment to decipher and navigate to where God is trying to take you. Along the way, watch out for counterfeits. Often, there will be paths you can follow that *seem* to line up with your gifts but aren't really the path for you.

I knew a gifted athlete with a passion for football who wanted to play in the NFL. He trained hard every day, and in addition to his physical abilities, he had gifts of determination, resilience, perseverance, and consistency. However, even with his hard work and dedication, his dream career as a football player on an NFL team didn't materialize. As he entered his late thirties, he held on to his dream, even though it was clearly not his calling. You don't have to know a lot about sports to know the NFL isn't drafting players pushing forty years old. That dream turned out to be a counterfeit, and because he held on to it for so long, it distracted him from finding his true calling. There are limitless other ways he can use the gifts God gave him, but until he stops chasing that counterfeit, he will struggle to find the work he should be doing.

That's not to say answering your calling will always come easily to you. While your gift comes naturally, putting it to work in your calling often requires effort and obedience. I was called to be an attorney, but my path to this career wasn't always easy. I faced obstacles all along the way. Because I never reached a dead end, because my gifts were in alignment with a career in the law, and because I knew I could fulfill my true purpose of glorifying God, I persevered. My wife is called to be a midwife. Achieving this goal requires study and work on her part. She's pursuing this vocation because it allows her to use her gifts, serve people, and become more Christlike in the process, but it's not effortless.

A lot of preachers and teachers get so deep with the idea of calling that people get confused. They start to think they have to get a direct message from God to know what their calling is. But it doesn't have to be that deep. Your calling may be realized over time, as you discover it through different experiences and exposure to people, vocations, and circumstances. You might find your calling in something that frustrates you, a situation you realize you can fix or improve upon. Your calling may show up in an unexpected opportunity or when you see a need and look to fill it, and your calling may change over time.

If you haven't yet found your calling, know that you're no less valuable than someone who's been doing what you think your calling may be for decades. You're no less valuable than the person who has a bigger following than you or seems to have impacted more people than you. Have confidence in yourself and your ability to do what God has called you to do. Know who you are in Christ, and be open to using your gift in the way God is calling you to, not just the way you desire.

Your gifts are inside you. No matter the challenges you've faced, you have something to offer to the world. You are worth something. You are valuable. Don't allow your gifts to lie dormant inside you. Ask God to empower you to maximize your potential, and while you pray for God's blessing on your efforts, keep pushing toward what God has created you to do. Do his will and give him the glory, and God will bless you and your gifts.

INDISPENSABLE ACTION STEPS
GIFTS

In a notebook or journal set aside for your leadership development, answer the following questions/complete the following exercises.

Assess.
Everyone has gifts. Make a list of the skills that have come naturally to you, including those you may have left behind in childhood. Include everything. No gift is too small.

Decide.
Make a list of the activities, work, and causes you feel passionate about.

What do you feel called to do?

Act.
Look for the overlap and connections between your gifts, your passions, and your calling.

VISION

I can do all this through him who gives me strength.
Philippians 4:13, NIV

I N 2006, I graduated from the University of North Carolina School of Law and immediately devoted myself to preparing for the bar examination. Every law school graduate must take and pass the bar exam to become a practicing attorney. This was no surprise, of course, but in my heart of hearts, I was concerned about how I would do on the test. My law school education felt incomplete. For three years, my professors had pushed me onward from one class to the next; however, I never felt like I had a good grasp on what I needed to know. I'd performed well enough to graduate, but I never got the sense that anyone cared if I learned anything. In the end, I felt unprepared to face the world as an attorney and ill-equipped to sit for the bar exam.

Regardless of my feelings about my law school experience, my goal was to become an attorney, and the only way to do that was to pass the bar. I buckled down, and for two months, I studied ten to fourteen hours a day. It's nearly impossible to hold down a job while preparing for the bar, so instead of trying to work, I exceeded the recommended study time. I was committed to the goal and determined to make up for any deficiencies in my law school education. I put aside just about everything else in my life. I paid the $600 fee for the exam. I showed up, and I did my best. And I failed.

When I saw my test results—after putting in so much work and investing money I didn't really have to spend—I fell to my knees. I couldn't figure out what I'd done wrong, and not knowing just made me that much more upset with myself. Even more so, I was angry with God. I'd honestly expected him to pull me through. After all, I'd honored God throughout my years of law school. I'd been intentional about showing people how good God was. I'd given him all the glory. I'd been obedient, and he'd let me fail in front of everyone.

I made sure God knew how disappointed I was, but as much as I railed, God never answered me or my questions. His silence only infuriated me more. "You don't have anything to say to me?" I asked him. Still, nothing.

Because I wasn't working, my brother had allowed me to stay with him. However, he had his own life and responsibilities, and it wasn't long before he asked me to contribute to the rent. I needed his support more than ever, but he was going through his own challenges and couldn't make me and my problems his priority. The temp jobs I picked up didn't pay much money, and because I couldn't give my brother what he asked for, I needed to find somewhere else to stay. My parents would have let me come home, but at twenty-six years old, I didn't want to move back in with my mother and father.

With my options dwindling, I moved in with my uncle, who was kind enough to give me a place to stay, and I prepared to take the bar again. During this time, I also grew closer to God. I had greater encounters with him, and I knew God was with me when the time came for me to sit for the bar exam a second time. By then, the wounds to my pride had healed. I'd made peace with not passing on the first try. I wasn't alone. Many attorneys—including such famous leaders as President Franklin D. Roosevelt, Secretary of State Hillary Clinton, and New York City Mayor Ed Koch—had taken the bar more than once, so I wasn't in bad company. It was a humbling experience, but I was ready to take the exam again and get started in my career.

I took the bar exam again, and again, I failed.

In fact, three times in a row, I failed to pass the test. Three times in a row, I came close to achieving my goal, only to have it snatched away from me. I was out of money and tired of sacrificing to study so intensely only to be disappointed again. I made up my mind that there wouldn't be a fourth time. Instead, I ordered brochures from different graduate school programs and tried to find a new path, maybe something in government or politics.

During this season, a gentleman from my church, an elder, was mentoring me, and one day, I shared with him my plan to give up on the law. As we drove along on our way to lunch, I told him, "God obviously doesn't want me to be a lawyer. I need to do something else."

The elder got quiet for a moment. Then he asked me, "How much would it cost to retake the test?"

I explained the fee was $400 every time I retook the exam, but I also had to pay for a hotel to stay near the testing center. The expenses added up quickly, and I was tapped out.

That night at Bible study, the elder called me to a back office. "Hold out your hand," he said. I did, and he pulled out a stack of cash and counted it into my open palm. When he was done counting, he looked at me and said, "I believe in you. Take the test again."

In that moment, a new energy coursed through me like shockwaves, bringing my vision back to life. Hearing those words of faith created in me a new sense of confidence. My mother, who had her doctorate, had always encouraged us to pursue education, but I hadn't heard that "I believe in you" message much from my father as I grew up. He didn't often express himself in that way, and so when the elder looked me in the face, man to man, and said those words, it meant more to me than he could've known. His quiet vote of confidence and his willingness to back it up by investing in me snapped me out of my pessimism.

After a falling out, my relationship with my parents had started to mend, and I went to visit them. I told my mom what had transpired between the elder and me, and she listened without comment. When I was done, she nodded and called me back to her bedroom. There, my mother took out her checkbook and wrote me a check for $1,000. "Nobody's ever going to believe in my son more than I believe in my son," she said as she pressed the check in my hand.

The elder supported me, my parents supported me, and Lauren, whom I'd met by this time, supported me. I had enough money to pay the exam fees, stay in a hotel, and not have to skimp on meals while I was there. With so much encouragement and assistance, I believed I could finally pass the exam. I committed to taking it one more time, but I told God, "I'm not taking it again. We pass this time, or I'm done."

Before the first day of the two-day test, a group of people at our church, including Lauren, came together to fast and pray for me. Later, several of them would tell me it was one of the hardest fasts they'd ever done. Some of them experienced headaches, some stomachaches, and some suffered both. The show of faith meant a lot when they shared it with me, but I had no idea what they were going through at the time. At the testing center, I was anxious and excited and ready to finally pass the bar and become a licensed attorney.

Two months later, I received the envelope with my scores inside. I ripped it open only to find a message saying my scores had been withheld. On both days of the exam, I'd somehow forgotten to leave my wallet behind in the hotel room. Since test takers are only allowed to bring in a pencil and an ID, I'd handed my wallet over to one of the attorneys overseeing the exam each day. My wallet had never crossed the threshold into the exam room, but someone had reported me for violating policy. The North Carolina State Bar gave me thirty days to respond and request a hearing.

Several people recommended I hire an attorney to represent me, but knowing I'd done nothing wrong, I decided to speak for myself. Before the hearing, I prayed and asked for guidance, and God gave me very specific instructions not to argue with anyone in that room. He directed me to be respectful and apologetic instead. "So you can talk now, God?" I thought. For so long, God had been quiet while I wandered through this wilderness, and when he chose to speak, he didn't answer any of my questions. His only words for me were to keep my mouth shut.

On that fateful day, most of the attorneys treated me with respect, but one of them came after me as if I were a criminal. His colleagues looked at him as if they wanted to tell him to calm down; however, no one dared. Angry thoughts raced through my mind as he sneered and called my intentions into question. I thought of all kinds of comebacks, but I remembered what God had told me. Against my own instincts, I answered each of that man's questions with "Yes, sir" and "No, sir" and left it at that. When he asked if I had anything to say for myself, I responded, "Thank you all for meeting with me. I apologize for my actions. They were unacceptable, and I promise you I won't conduct myself that way as an attorney." At the end of the day, my career was in their hands—assuming, of course, that I'd passed the bar this time.

I waited weeks to receive a decision. Finally, I arrived home in the pouring rain one day and found the envelope in my mailbox. I stood there, soaking wet, while a friend who had given me a ride waited to get the news. I opened the envelope, and the letter read: "We have decided to release your scores. Congratulations." I read that far, and then I screamed and hollered. I praised God until it stopped raining, the clouds broke, and the sun shone in the sky. Neighbors came out on their balconies and smiled and laughed as they watched me. Finally, someone asked what I was so excited about, and I shouted, "I passed the North Carolina bar exam! I'm going to be an attorney!"

Law school was three years of hard work and struggle. Many people had warned me not to even attempt it because, they said, too many people failed at it or succeeded but at too high a cost. Taking the bar not just once or twice but four times before I passed required months of financial sacrifice, arduous studying, and surviving and overcoming disappointment after disappointment. Going into that hearing and keeping my mouth shut while an attorney who didn't know me unfairly attacked my character required discipline and obedience to God. None of that would've been possible for me without a clear vision of my future as an attorney.

A leader cannot lead without a vision. In order to lead yourself or whoever is following you, you must have a destination. Your vision is like the address you put into your GPS. Without that address, you can look at the map on your screen all day, but it won't take you where you need to go. It's impossible to create anything in your life without a vision for it. You have to see it to seize it. Without a vision, your calling will go unanswered and your purpose unfulfilled. The people who want to support you won't know how to step in to help you build because they won't know what you're building. Leaders create a vision that they and anyone who chooses to follow or support them can work to make a reality.

WRITE THE VISION AND MAKE IT PLAIN

You must have a clearly defined vision—this is the second key to leadership—but to bring it to fruition, you need to do more than just write down what you want. Figuring out *how* you'll make it happen is an essential part of this process. You need a plan. You need to know the steps to take to get to your destination. Those steps will become your goals along the way to making your vision come true.

Whenever you set out to accomplish something new, start by doing your research. Someone, somewhere, has already done it—or at least, they've done something comparable—and you can learn from their successes and failures. Other people have launched businesses, started ministries, gotten promotions, raised great kids, and done just about anything you can imagine doing. You don't have to reinvent the wheel. Instead, learn from their experience by seeking mentorship. While personal mentor-mentee relationships can serve you well, they're not required for you to have mentors and benefit from their expertise. Anyone can be your mentor when you read their books, watch their videos, take their courses, or attend their conferences and seminars. Use what you learn to formulate your plan, and hire a coach or consultant to guide you when you need more specific feedback or guidance.

Finally, ask God to bless your vision and give you the wisdom you need to create the plan. Continue to go to him in prayer as you execute the steps laid out before you. Ask for the right words to say in meetings and negotiations. Pray for the discernment to make good decisions and to recognize the people best suited to help you achieve your goals. Be open to hearing what God has to say about your plan even if he tells you to change it.

ALWAYS HAVE A PLAN B

When I was a young man, my father was the pastor of a small church, which he founded. He didn't have much success, as many people would define it, in growing his church. Membership didn't expand much, and he never moved into his own church building. We held services in a day care center, and some of the people from the church he formerly attended would occasionally come to visit. Sometimes, they'd walk in and snicker. They mocked the fact that he didn't have a building and they belittled his efforts.

While those naysayers may not have seen growth they could measure, my dad followed his vision. Whether anyone else knew it or not, his church had at least one positive impact when I got saved under him at eighteen years old. Under his leadership, I found a desire within me to understand the Word more deeply. I decided to live a Christian life, and I began to study the sermons of great pastors.

Not long after I was saved, my dad preached a message that has stayed with me and influences how I live to this day. There may have been five worshipers in church that Sunday, but my father didn't let the small turnout water down his message. That day, he talked about goals, and he left us with three simple points. My dad explained that in order to accomplish anything that matters, you have to set your goals, work toward them, and prepare for opposition. For me, that message hit home. It was a model that got me through college, law school, the bar, and beyond.

Many of us know we have to set and work toward our goals, but too often, we fail to factor in the opposition we'll inevitably face. I have a great life. I've achieved a lot, but I still face opposition, and I have at every step of the way. I'm very blessed; however, my awareness that opposition is always coming keeps me prepared for it. When I experience backbiting and backstabbing in that small percentage of my life, I'm not thrown off. It may come from somewhere unexpected, but the fact that it comes doesn't surprise me, and I bounce back quickly and better than before. The enemy doesn't want to see my law firm grow or my church in its own building. I understand this, and because I do, I've prepared myself for the challenges to come. I'm equipped to handle that opposition.

It's one thing to say, "Haters gonna hate" and another thing entirely to experience it. If you're not ready, it will knock you off your game and distract you from your vision. Too many people get caught off guard by any little pushback they face along the way as they pursue their vision. They don't expect hate from the people in their own circles. They aren't prepared for circumstances going any way other than the way they want, so when obstacles rise in front of them, they question the vision. They doubt their ability to fulfill it. They even question their own worth. Because they expected everyone to be on their side and all decisions to be made in their favor, they give up too soon and too easily.

Once you have a vision and a plan to make it happen, understand that things won't go exactly as you planned. Life just doesn't happen that way, which is why a good leader always has a plan B. Many people don't like to talk about backup plans because they think it means giving up on their vision altogether, but that's not necessarily the case. Yes, there are times when going to your plan B means changing your destination, but even when you're still headed to the same place, you may need to take a different route.

Your plan B should describe how you'll go over, under, around, or through any obstacle to achieve your vision. To design this plan, sit down and brainstorm every potential problem you might face, including your own internal resistance or weaknesses. Is there a character trait you need to develop further to make it possible to achieve your goal? Are you lacking any necessary skills? If your vision has a budget, is it possible you'll fall short on your funding or go over budget? If your vision has a clear deadline, what will you do if you see it drawing near and you're behind schedule? Who might interfere with your plans? What environmental, economic, or social events might stand in your way?

Once you've identified all the obstacles you can reasonably think of, it's time to define what action you can take to prevent them and what you'll do if they actually come up for you. You won't be able to predict or prevent every possible obstacle, but thinking through many of them will prepare you to respond quickly when faced with unexpected challenges. Don't shy away from this process. It will only make you stronger and improve your odds of achieving your vision.

BE FAITHFUL AND CONSISTENT

When I was just an infant, my parents held me up before God and asked him to bless me and make me an attorney one day. They even called me "the attorney" when I was a baby. They believed the law would be a good path for me, and they prayed for me to find it. Although they didn't tell me about that moment until I was an adult, I began to say I wanted to be an attorney in elementary school. I didn't know it, but I was developing the same vision for myself that my parents had held for me from the beginning of my life.

During my sophomore year in high school, I spent many afternoons watching television clips of renowned attorney Johnnie Cochran successfully defending O. J. Simpson. Observing the workings of a courtroom gave me a sense of the reality of criminal law. The trial lasted eleven months and dominated the news for much of that time. Most people thought we were watching a celebrity on his way to prison, but Mr. Cochran's skills and experience outmatched his opponents' abilities, and he led a legal dream team that destroyed the prosecution. Even if you believed the defendant was guilty, you had to admit Johnnie Cochran owned that courtroom. Watching him argue his case, I saw the kind of lawyer I wanted to be.

I don't know exactly what my parents imagined for me when they asked God to make me an attorney. I doubt they pictured everything I went through to get here because unless you've walked it, understanding the reality of any path can be difficult. When I watched Mr. Cochran in the courtroom, I didn't have any idea what kind of work he'd put in to become the attorney he was by then. I had no clue what challenges he might have faced along the way. I only saw a man at the height of his profession.

Even now, my life as an attorney isn't exactly how I imagined it would be. However, it has brought me many of the benefits and opportunities I expected, and many I never anticipated, because I remained faithful to the vision. It wasn't always easy, but I stayed consistent with what I said I wanted to achieve. I struggled through law school and sacrificed the salary I could've been earning in another field during the time I worked to pass the bar. Even as an attorney, I had employers who didn't always recognize my value. Since I opened my own practice, I've had employees quit and leave me short-staffed during some of my busiest seasons, but at no point did I decide it was too hard. At no point did I give up.

You cannot allow a setback to paralyze you. Instead, make the best decision you can make in the moment, get back on track with the plan, or enact your plan B. Don't think you'll step away from your vision and come back to it later either, because starting and stopping kills momentum. If you want to realize your vision, you have to be faithful and consistent in pursuing your goals. You have to keep moving forward. Do not give up.

THINK BIGGER

Recently, a potential client called me and shared that, although he'd found several attorneys who offered free consultations, he opted to pay to consult with me instead. "First impressions are big for me," he explained. He'd done his research, and my website stood out from the others. In his opinion, my site was more polished than many he'd come across. He also noticed I'd received dozens of positive reviews from satisfied clients, while many of the other attorneys he checked out only had a few. Given everything he'd seen, he chose to go with me.

As I listened to his assessment of my online presence, I smiled to myself. Everything he described I'd created intentionally. I place a high importance on doing my job well, but appearances also matter, so I've expanded my thinking beyond continuously honing my craft. I combine my standard for excellence in how I represent my clients with a high standard of excellence in how my firm presents itself. For example, I work with funnel experts and search engine optimization experts to help more potential clients find my website. That's an investment in my business, so when people land on my site, I need to give them a reason to stay there and to call my office. That starts with what they see.

Some people believe being good at your profession should be enough and your ability should speak for itself. While that sounds good, it's not the way the real world works. Many people will judge you before they have any idea whether you're the best chef, the best photographer, the best dentist, restauranteur, manager, or attorney. Winning people—clients, customers, followers, and supporters—over to your vision requires you to think bigger than what your vision will deliver for them. You also have to think about how people will know about it and how they'll perceive it on its face.

If you want to lead your frontline employees to better performance, you need to gain their respect by looking like someone they should follow. If you want to lead your family to live a healthier lifestyle, you'll have an easier time getting them to agree if you look like the picture of health and radiate the benefits of those lifestyle changes. The fact is, as a leader, you're constantly selling your vision to other people. When they believe in you, they're much more likely to get on board and support you. Ultimately, that won't be because of how you look or how fancy your website is. Your integrity, faithfulness to the vision, and good decisions will cause your followers to stick with you. However, the way you represent the vision will get their attention and attract them to you in the first place.

To think bigger and see your vision realized, you must become your own best advocate. As a leader, you'll often be called to advocate on behalf of your followers. Before you can do that, you have to make it a habit to advocate for yourself. Don't let anyone devalue your worth. Sometimes we're afraid to speak up about our prices in our business, the salary we deserve, or the promotion we should have received last year. Begin to recognize the value of your time, money, wisdom, and experience, and require others to value them too.

Thinking bigger also requires a willingness to evolve in your vision. Leaders continue to take on new challenges, learning and growing even as they achieve one success after another. As one version of their vision comes to fruition, they expand on it because no leader can ever claim to have completely mastered their field. If you own a business, you can evolve as an entrepreneur by offering new products or services, reaching new target markets, creating strategic partnerships, or simply by finding new efficiencies. As a professional or a tradesperson, you can take classes and earn new certifications. Parents can grow by reading books on communication or sibling rivalry or by talking with more experienced parents.

There's no limit to the ways you can develop as a leader, and that development should never end. As you grow, your vision will grow with you and may far exceed what you believe it to be today.

INDISPENSABLE ACTION STEPS
VISION

In a notebook or journal set aside for your leadership development, answer the following questions/complete the following exercises.

1. Craft your vision for your life five years in the future and ten years in the future.
2. Draft a plan for how you will bring this vision to life by brainstorming a list of steps that will get you there.
   a. How long will each step take?
   b. How much time can you reasonably afford to dedicate to each step?
   c. How much will it cost?
   d. How much money do you have available?
   e. How can you acquire any additional capital you may need?
   f. Do you have the necessary skills to complete each task?
   g. Can you learn what you need to know, or does it make more sense to hire an expert?
   h. Where do you need help?
3. Create your plan B by answering the following questions. (Keep in mind that you may need a plan C, D, and E as new obstacles arise.)
   a. What character trait do you need to develop further to make it possible to achieve your goal?

b. Are you lacking any necessary skills? How can you develop those skills or find someone else to provide them?

c. If your vision has a budget, is it possible you'll fall short on your funding or go over budget? How can you prevent or deal with this possibility?

d. If your vision has a clear deadline, what will you do if you see it drawing near and you're behind schedule?

e. Who might interfere with your plans?

f. What environmental, economic, or social events might stand in your way?

Take one action today toward making your vision a reality.

INTEGRITY

Now the overseer is to be above reproach, faithful to his wife,
temperate, self-controlled, respectable, hospitable, able to teach.
1 Timothy 3:2, NIV

NOT FAR FROM my home is a gas station I used to frequent on my daily commute. It was convenient, but each time I stopped there, I got a racist vibe from the employees, who were all White. They made it clear they didn't appreciate me entering their space. Inside the convenience store, I'd greet them with, "Hey, y'all. How you doing?" And their response was always the same. Not a word. Not a nod or wave in my direction. None of the Southern hospitality they offered to the White customers who came in while I was there.

One day, I stopped at the gas station on my way home from work, and as always, I greeted the cashier. She took my money but couldn't be bothered to speak. "Fine," I thought. "I'm done giving these people my money." I was ready to leave, but as the cashier slid my change across the counter to me—careful not to touch my hand—I saw she'd accidentally given me a hundred-dollar bill.

I was done shopping there, since they clearly didn't appreciate my patronage, and I would never see that clerk again. I could've slid that hundred in my wallet and walked out the door, and she wouldn't have known until she counted out her register at the end of the day. Even then, she probably wouldn't have realized she'd given the money to me. In that moment, because she'd been consistently nasty to me, I wanted to keep the cash. "That's what you get for being so disrespectful and rude," I thought. "Maybe God's trying to teach you a lesson and give me a blessing at the same time." But deep inside, the idea wasn't quite resonating with my conscience.

I was so tempted to keep the money, but I could hear the Holy Spirit telling me to give it back. In that moment, I had a choice to make. "Ma'am," I said, "I think you miscounted." I slid the money back to her.

The clerk looked at the change she'd given me, and seeing the hundred-dollar bill, she glanced at her coworker and back at me as her face flushed red. "Oh, well, thank you," she said, barely able to get the words out.

I went back to that store a couple more times, and I was treated with begrudging politeness, as if I'd finally earned the right to basic human dignity. I did stop shopping there, but I never regretted returning the money. It was the right thing to do. It was the only choice I could make and be in integrity with who I say I am. Regardless of how they'd treated me, I remained the same person. My character in dealing with the employees at that store was unimpeachable.

In the legal system, a witness whose testimony is reliable and credible, whose character is trustworthy, and whose behavior is beyond reproach is unimpeachable. Effective leaders strive to live an unimpeachable life. If you want people to follow you, they have to be able to trust you. If you want to achieve success in your personal life, your spouse, children, and family have to be able to depend on you to keep your word. In your professional life, clients, colleagues, subordinates, and superiors must think of you as someone who can be trusted to do what you say you're going to do and to live by the values you claim to hold.

A call to integrity is not a call to perfection. No one is perfect. However, you can strive for excellence in all things. You can choose to live and act with integrity—doing the right thing, at all times, even when no one else will know and even when doing the wrong thing might feel good or benefit you in the moment. To create meaningful success in your life, you must uphold your moral principles even when it's hard, even when it costs you in the short term.

Integrity is the third leadership key, and like the others, it's essential to succeeding in any real or meaningful way. We've all seen how much a lack of integrity can cost. Broken marriages, ruined relationships, failed businesses, and prison sentences all frequently result from a lack of integrity. You might manage to execute some version of your vision, but you won't be able to sustain it without integrity. If you use your gifts for good instead of evil, you're in integrity. If you execute your vision with as much concern for the people around you as for yourself, you're in integrity. Leaders walk in integrity.

KNOW YOUR BOUNDARIES AND LIVE BY THEM

Certain professions are held to a higher standard of ethical behavior under the law. Elected officials, doctors, members of the military, and lawyers all swear an oath of some sort as a public declaration of their willingness to uphold that standard. These are positions of power, and with that power comes an additional level of responsibility. These professions are all leadership roles, and in different ways, these professionals are entrusted with people's lives. When they behave out of alignment with the standards of their profession, the consequences can be devastating. This is why people are often incensed to find out a doctor has been peddling prescriptions for opioids, a judge has taken bribes, or a president is suspected of breaking the law. This is why we're rightfully outraged by police officers who are entrusted with a badge and then abuse the power that badge gives them.

Some professionals can lose their right to practice their profession if they act outside of integrity. Physicians, attorneys, veterinarians, accountants, and other professionals whose ability to practice is regulated by governing bodies can be sued for professional malpractice. If they're found to have been negligent or incompetent in their work, they can be held accountable. Essentially, they hold themselves out as experts, and they are expected to behave as such, but there's an ethical component to their accountability. Acting unethically can cost these professionals their reputation and their livelihood.

Many people don't have a defined code of ethics in their job, but you don't need anyone to give you rules to follow. Set these ethical standards for yourself. Set firm boundaries and live by them at work, at home, and everywhere in between. Don't wait for someone else to hold you to the highest ethical standards. Choose to walk in integrity. Be a leader you can respect. Be a leader people want to follow. That's what makes you a leader in your own life. That's how you'll create success.

DON'T COMPROMISE FOR SUCCESS

When I went to visit a friend and drove up to his mini mansion, I was in awe. Knocking on the door, I kept thinking I must have the wrong address. This couldn't possibly be his house. We had only graduated high school about ten years earlier, and I had just passed the bar and was getting started in my career. My friend, who I'll call Darryl, opened the door and let me into his beautiful home. As he gave me a quick tour, Darryl explained he was ordering new furniture from overseas and renovating some of the rooms.

I respected what he seemed to have achieved for himself, but I also felt somewhat intimidated and even slightly insecure about my rate of progress in life. But he had reached out to me as a friend, and I decided to let my guard down, let go of the jealousy, and humble myself to learn from him. Clearly, he knew something I didn't about creating wealth. I put my ego aside and tried to be open-minded, and I didn't have to wait long for Darryl to explain how he'd come to live such a lavish lifestyle.

We sat down at a table, and Darryl explained to me that he was an entrepreneur. He invested in real estate and his business was a huge success. As he talked, I sat up and listened closely. I wanted to get every word of the wisdom he was dropping.

"Micah," Darryl said, "I'm going to make you a millionaire, but don't you ever tell anybody how I did it." He went on to ask me what I thought people like Bill Gates, Lebron James, and Warren Buffett had in common. They were all at the top of their fields and incredibly rich and successful, but I couldn't see any other similarities. Darryl explained that those men and others like them shared more than that. He said they'd all had to do "something" to get to the top. He hinted at something corrupt; however, that was as far as he went. I didn't know what he wanted to say about those men, but I was eager to learn more about how I could create my own wealth.

From what I could see, this man had so much of what I wanted. I would've loved to live in a mansion I could decorate with high-end furniture. I would've loved to have the money to make my parents' life more comfortable and buy them small luxuries. I would've loved to have a wealthy life at such a young age, even before I got married. In that moment, I decided I would learn all I could from Darryl.

In the following weeks, however, I saw another side of my old high school friend. I left his house pumped and ready to earn my millions, but when I introduced him to Lauren, who I was dating at that time, she was completely unimpressed. She looked past the big house and saw something in him that she didn't trust. I wanted Lauren to get involved in his business along with me, and I explained that the business had made him a millionaire. "Good for him," said Lauren, but she wanted no part of it. His warning, "Don't you ever tell anybody how I did it," replayed in my mind, yet I saw no reason not to pursue the venture.

One day, I saw Darryl at church, and I introduced him to a friend of mine. Darryl told us he was hosting an event at his place and I was invited. "Tell your boy he can come too," he said. But there was such arrogance in the way he spoke to us. Right there in church, my friend blurted out an expletive and said, "I'm not going to his house after he talked to me like that." I agreed with him that there was something off about the way Darryl had approached us, as if he were doing us a big favor, letting us in on something exclusive even though he thought we were somehow beneath him.

When I told Lauren about the conversation, she wasn't the least bit surprised by it, and this time I listened to her. I valued her opinion then as I still do. Lauren is a good judge of character and can often see things I overlook. She wasn't blinded by his material wealth, and following her counsel, I cut ties with Darryl. I'd later be glad I did.

When Darryl offered me the opportunity to earn vast sums of money by working with him, I could have overlooked his questionable behavior and the unanswered questions about how he'd become so rich so quickly. Some people would say I should have taken the opportunity and run with it. However, the cracks were showing in Darryl's character. Even though building wealth was important to me, and by all appearances he knew how to do that, working with him would've required me to compromise my values.

Years later, I crossed paths with a young woman who had partnered with Darryl on a business venture. During our conversation, I asked about Darryl and their work together. "He has so much wealth and success. How did he do it so fast?" I asked.

The woman stared at me for a minute, and then she described how Darryl had made most of his money on the wrong side of the law. He'd saved tens of thousands of dollars over the years, and he had made some attempts to go legitimate with that money. But the streets kept calling him and he kept going back.

I had never known that side of Darryl. When he asked me what all those successful men had in common, I can only think now that he meant they'd all had some illegitimate start to their business—that they'd used dirty money or somehow cheated the system. I have no reason to believe that's true, but perhaps it made him sleep better at night to believe he was just doing what all successful people did. Maybe it was his way of letting me know what I could expect if I went into business with him.

It can be tempting to compromise your integrity to get what you want. I'm forty-two, and while I have a successful business, I don't have a seven-figure bank balance. If I had gone into business with Darryl, I might have that kind of wealth now. Or I might have lost everything. Either way, I'd have to live every day knowing I had compromised the standards I set for myself and those God has for me. I would have compromised my integrity in the name of success. Fortunately, God and the woman who would become my wife kept me from an association that could have cost me much more than it was worth in the long run.

We all want success, and it comes at a price. You may have to sacrifice time, money, and even some relationships along the way.

But when you sacrifice the values you claim to live by, when you sacrifice your integrity, the cost of success is much too high.

GIVE 100% IN EVERYTHING YOU DO

My mom and dad were always hard workers, and while they never sat me down and told me I should be a hard worker too, I learned from their example. When I was fifteen years old, my brother helped me get a job at the grocery store where he worked, and I gave that job 100 percent of my effort on every shift I worked. I started as a bagger, and between customers, I was constantly running outside to bring the carts back. It didn't matter if it was hot outside, or if I was tired, or even if the other baggers were slacking. My job was to keep the carts in, and I made sure it got done.

As soon as I turned sixteen, the store manager promoted me to cashier, and I quickly found my groove there. I figured out how to scan groceries in one continuous motion, so I became the fastest cashier in the store. It didn't take long for me to develop a reputation among the customers as the cashier who could get you out fast. Even when I had a long line, customers would get in my line because they knew I would still get them out faster than someone who only had a couple of customers waiting. In fact, I scanned so fast that some customers asked me to slow down so they could see the prices. If they wanted a slow cashier, they had picked the wrong one. I was focused on producing. At the end of the day, my drawer would be stacked with cash and the count would always be spot on. At sixteen years old, I earned an award as cashier of the month.

Even though working at a grocery store wasn't my dream job, I gave it 100 percent. Some jobs are just a stepping-stone or a training ground, but as a leader, you must still give that job 100 percent of your effort while you're doing it. That's how you develop the skills and mentality you'll need to take you where you want to go. How you do the small assignments is how you will do the big assignments. If you want God to bless you with a promotion, give your all to the job you have today. If you want God to bless you with your own business, give your current boss your full effort while you're at work. Even if you don't feel appreciated, fulfilling your commitment is how you do your job with integrity.

Choose to become a person who gives 100 percent in every area of your life, and you can live a life of no regrets. If your marriage comes to an end after you've done everything you could to make it work, you can still hold your head up. If your child makes a poor decision, but you know your all went into raising that child to do the right thing, then you can live with a clean conscience. If you're fired from your job, but you can honestly say you gave your all each day, then you can walk away knowing you've been a good steward of God's blessings.

When you give 100 percent, you inspire other people to do the same. It doesn't matter what your role is. You lead by example whether you're bagging groceries or own the store. You model a strong work ethic for the people in your circles of influence, which opens the way for them to raise the standard for their own work. Your effort contributes to the greater good, and at the same time, it helps you develop into your next level of leadership.

DEMONSTRATE YOUR VALUE AND YOUR VALUES

As a leader, you're always contributing to the betterment of not just your own situation but whatever circumstances you find yourself in. Your presence and participation provide value to the people and organizations you interact with and belong to at any point in time. In order for you to be in integrity, your decisions must align with your values. Simply put, every place you spend time should be made better by your presence and contributions.

Leaders provide value in these four ways wherever they go:

1. Leaders solve problems.
2. Leaders lead by example.
3. Leaders lead with compassion.
4. Leaders lead with the right motives.

Leaders solve problems. Problem-solving requires you to become mentally tough and develop the discipline to keep going when things don't go your way. Leaders bring ideas to the table, but you have to keep in mind that every problem won't be solved with the first solution you come up with. Leaders don't quit until they find a solution that works. When you develop a mindset of positive thinking and a habit of positive self-talk, you begin to see every problem has a solution of some sort. You can change the circumstances, change how you react to the circumstances, or change how you feel about the circumstances.

If you want to be average, if you want to be a follower, then do what the average person does. Most people will either complain about a problem or decide there's nothing they can do about it. They'll live with it until the situation gets bad enough and the pain of the problem grows so great that they finally feel motivated to do something about it. Leaders don't wait for problems to get progressively worse. As a leader, you identify the problem and take action to solve it as quickly as possible.

Here are seven steps for effective problem-solving:

1. Accept that you have this challenge and clearly define the problem.
2. Have faith that God has given you the resources you need, and believe in your ability to solve the problem.

3.   Assess what you've done wrong and what you've done right up to this point.
4.   Choose a new approach, or to continue in the same direction, based on that evaluation.
5.   Turn to mentors for advice and feedback on your plan.
6.   Make a decision and take action, one step at a time, to execute on your decision.
7.   Repeat this process until the problem is resolved.

Leaders lead by example. When I worked at the grocery store, I wasn't in management. I was in frontline positions. But even as a bagger, I was able to set an example for other baggers, for cashiers, and for managers. No one reported to me, but everyone could see my strong work ethic and my drive. If anyone was even a little bit inspired by the work I put in, then I was, in fact, serving them in a leadership capacity. Just know there's always someone watching you. Sometimes, it's a person who needs to learn from you. Sometimes, it's a person who sees your hard work and wants to reward it. God is watching all the time and will bless your efforts.

As an attorney, I set an example for my clients in the way I fight for them, always in an ethical manner. As a pastor, I lead by example by showing up for my congregation every Sunday and Wednesday and never asking anyone to do more than I'm willing to do. As a father, I lead by example with every word and action my children hear or see. You have the same ability to lead by example in every role you play at work or school, at home, at church, and even in your public interactions.

Strive to be the best example of whatever you're gifted and graced to do. Your gifts come from God, by the grace of God. While you may not always be the best at that gift, in a competitive sense, you can always lead by example by being the best possible model of a good steward of your gifts. If you've been given a gift for visual arts, speaking, performing, or caregiving—whatever your gift may be—use it fully and for the glory of God.

Leaders lead with compassion. You can't forget about the people you want to follow you. You can't roll over people in your pursuit of success. When you have the opportunity, give individualized attention and care to the people who look up to you. At the same time, have compassion for the leaders you follow in any area of your life. You may not have the full picture of everything your boss, your pastor, or the leader of your favorite organization has on his or her plate. However, seek to understand what they're going through. Pray for them to have the discernment to do God's will, and in whatever ways you can, support their efforts to do good. Your followers and supporters will see your compassion and reward you with the same.

Remember the first person you must lead is yourself. Treat yourself with the same compassion you show other people. Accept that you'll make mistakes along the way. You'll fail. You'll fall short. Don't waste time beating yourself up. Instead, assess where you went wrong. Correct your mistakes where you can and get help where you need it. Pray for the discernment to do God's will. Repent and forgive yourself when you stray from that path.

Lead with the right motives. We all desire a certain level of material success and comfort in our lives. There's nothing wrong with that. Money creates options for you and your family. Money can uplift your community and provide opportunities for people who otherwise wouldn't have them. Money can be used to do great good. However, if you allow money, or any other selfish purpose, to become your primary motivation, you're out of integrity. You have lost your way. We know this because the pursuit of money doesn't bring honor to God.

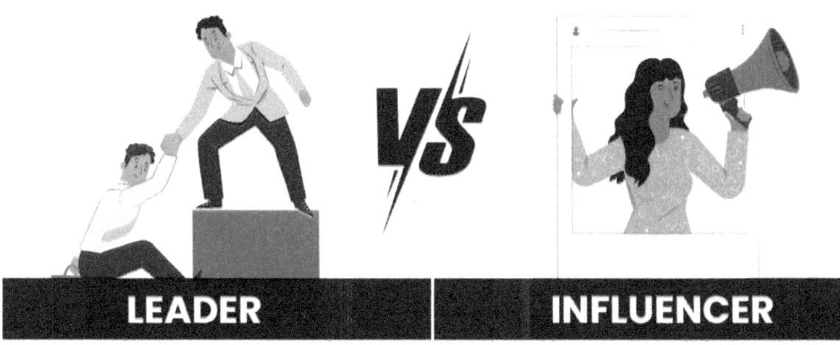

Whatever your mission is in life, profiting off people is never the right way to go about accomplishing it. Profiting from serving people, however, is an honorable motive. You have to actually care about what's in it for them. Author and speaker Zig Ziglar said, "You can have everything in life you want, if you will just help other people get what they want." The rewards of leading to serve are limitless. Be willing to walk people through to their next stage of development. Pour into those people coming up behind you and help them accomplish their own goals. Figure out how you can add more value in your circles of influence and do it.

While you should always have goals for yourself and what you'll accomplish, make sure you include others. When you pray for your own success, pray to provide more value. If you're praying people will buy your book, pray also that your book can be of service to more readers. If you're praying more people will come to your church service or buy from your business, pray also that you can touch more hearts or that more customers will be blessed by the product or service you offer. Remember you're here to use your God-given gifts to glorify God and serve other people. Stay focused on the mission, and the money will come. Money follows mission.

Integrity—staying in alignment with a moral code and doing the right thing even when nobody's looking—is essential to leadership because without integrity leaders become selfish, unreliable, and corrupt. For leaders who live in integrity, success is guaranteed because you define success differently than other people. You'll always ensure those who follow you also succeed. You'll always be able to look yourself in the mirror and be happy with what you see, knowing that everything you've achieved came to you the right way.

INDISPENSABLE ACTION STEPS
INTEGRITY

In a notebook or journal set aside for your leadership development, answer the following questions/complete the following exercises.

1. Create your personal code of ethics. Write out the boundaries you have or will set in your life and work.
2. Where have you compromised for success in your life at any point? What did you learn from that choice? How will you handle similar situations differently in the future?
3. At times, we all fall short on giving our best effort. In what part of your life do you need to refocus and start giving 100 percent?

PEOPLE

Humble yourselves before the Lord, and he will lift you up.
James 4:10, NIV

I N 2020, THE COVID-19 pandemic created a hectic lifestyle for our family, just as it did for so many people. Lauren, already a registered nurse, pressed her way through graduate school on her way to becoming a midwife. She also had our three kids at home and her ministry work on her plate. It wasn't easy, but she held it all down, and as her husband, I was incredibly proud of her focus and her progress. On my end, while we moved church services online, streamlining my pastoral duties, combined with my law practice, still placed demands on my time and mental energy.

During this time, I became acutely aware of the people on our team. Trusted friends and family members were supportive as always and are with us for life. Yet, I had to recognize other people were either for us or against us. Their presence either added to our lives in some way or it detracted from our lives. Very few people held a neutral place because, while it doesn't take much to contribute—a friendly greeting every day, a listening ear when things get tough—it doesn't take much to detract either. I upped my investment in mutually beneficial relationships and quietly stepped away from others.

I became more intentional than ever about finding the right team members for my businesses, the right supporters for my church, and the right experts to help me develop in the aspects of my life where I had significant goals. I hired a coach who specializes in pastoral leadership to give me guidance on how to manage my fledgling church during a pandemic. I hired a book coach to guide me in writing this book, and I hired a marketing coach to help me create marketing systems. As an ethical goal-achievement expert and leadership mentor, as an attorney and as a pastor, and as an author and speaker, I've accomplished a lot, but I have so much more I want to do. To get there, I want experts on my team.

As an adult, you have the power to choose who you permit to be a part of your life. Don't take these decisions lightly. There's always room for the people you love, even if they aren't exactly in alignment with your lifestyle or your values. I don't advocate viciously cutting people out of your life, especially when you could serve as the model they need to begin to live at a higher level. At the same time, most of the people in your life are there because you allow them to be. Choose people who can mentor and lead you. Choose people who will support you, personally and professionally, and who you can support in return. Choose wisely.

BE MINDFUL OF YOUR ASSOCIATIONS

When I was twelve years old, I lived across the street from four girls who lived with their grandparents. One day, while I was outside dribbling my basketball to pass the time, the girls called me over and invited me inside. They were home alone, and as I entered their dimly lit family room, the light from the television flickered and danced and strange sounds came from the set. The girls were all watching a show, but it wasn't Saturday morning cartoons or even soap operas. When I looked at the screen, I saw something I never expected to see.

Right there in front of us, naked men and naked women romped around. The girls smiled up at me, as if all this were perfectly normal. They shot me welcoming looks and invited me to watch the film with them. I'd never seen anything like it in my life. I was dumbfounded. I was surprised and confused not just by what I'd seen but also by the way these girls had no problem inviting me into their secret world. As far as I knew, they came from a Christian home, so they must have known better. I certainly knew this behavior went against everything I'd been taught. I should have spoken up, but out of fear and embarrassment, I didn't mention it to my parents or any other responsible adult.

Unfortunately, I was introduced to a new world of temptation on a VCR that day, and later, the Internet made it easier than ever to access indecent content. In my teen years, I hung out with a group of older guys who regularly gathered together to watch pornography, and I eventually developed a habit of watching it on my own. Something I knew in my spirit was wrong became a regular part of my life. I have no doubt that if I'd continued to associate with men or women who partook in pornography, I'd still be participating in the same behavior. Fortunately, I ended those associations, and by finding fulfillment in my faith and in healthy relationships, I cut pornography out of my life for good.

Many people in our society talk about how children and adolescents can fall in with the "wrong crowd" and develop bad habits and poor character because of those influences. They're absolutely right. I was a kid when that happened to me, and I was more susceptible to outside influences because of my lack of maturity. However, adults can also fall under the influence of peers, colleagues, friends, and associates. While you should have more judgment by the time you reach adulthood, other adults have also developed sophisticated skills of persuasion they can use to lead you down the wrong path.

For better or worse, the people you associate with have an influence on your life. If the people in your social circle think a little adultery is no big deal as long as no one finds out, you may start to think flirting with someone other than your spouse is OK. If your friends plan their weekends around smoking and drinking, your chances of doing the same drastically increase. If the folks you hang out with have no time for the gym and laugh at the idea of eating for health, it can be harder for you to avoid junk food and stick to your workouts.

When your parents told you, "Birds of a feather flock together," they were right. People often gravitate to people who are like them. This can be great when they all share the same positive values, but too often, it's because it makes them feel better about their own questionable choices. They enjoy seeing their own poor behavior reflected in their friends and associates because it can be uncomfortable to spend time with someone operating at a higher level. Complainers like to hang out with other people who complain. Slackers gravitate toward people who don't have much going on in their lives. Criminals tend to have friends who have no qualms about breaking the law.

When your grandparents told you, "If you lie down with dogs you get up with fleas," they were right too. You cannot expect to spend considerable time with people and not be influenced or impacted by their actions. Even if you never participate in the same behavior, you will suffer the consequences of it. People on the outside will look at you and assume you have the same values, and that you approve of your associates' unethical, immature, or immoral behavior.

Some people who enter your life will look like they share your values and have something to offer as your friend or associate, but don't be deceived by appearances. Keep an eye out for the following red flags.

Red flag #1. They trash talk their "friends" behind their backs. These people don't understand loyalty. If they're running a friend down to you today, they'll be ranting about your shortcomings to someone else tomorrow.

Red flag #2. They mistreat people—family members, service workers, or strangers—in front of you. People who don't have basic respect for a cashier or server, much less for their spouse or their children, are likely only giving you respect because they think they can get something from you. The day will come when they treat you the same way.

Red flag #3. Everything bad that's ever happened to them was someone else's fault. We've all been on the receiving end of someone else's bad decisions, but people who constantly feel victimized will drain your time and energy. Because they feel no responsibility for their results, they feel powerless and angry. Often, it's only a matter of time before something that goes wrong in their life is your fault too.

Red flag #4. They're quick to confess everything they've ever done wrong and tell you how they've changed. This can be a trick to disarm you and get you to trust them. Proceed with caution. Let time and their actions tell you how sincere their repentance really is.

Red flag #5. They live a "too good to be true" lifestyle, and they're vague about how they acquired all their material wealth. No one is required to share their income or their financial success strategies with you, but be wary of anyone who seems to live a life well beyond their means.

Red flag #6. They have no close friends or family you can meet. Some people have detached from their families to protect themselves from destructive relatives. In certain situations, that's reasonable. However, if you meet someone who has no one in their life—friend or family—who they trust and turn to for support and advice, be careful. There may be a good reason why no one wants to be close to them.

Red flag #7. They constantly talk about problems but never suggest solutions. They'd rather complain than do the work to bring about change. In fact, they may not even believe change is possible. When you suggest solutions, they give you all the reasons why those solutions are impossible for them. Run, don't walk, away from these people. If you don't, they'll drag you down into the quicksand of their negativity.

Red flag #8. They constantly name-drop and brag about their accomplishments. There's nothing wrong with sharing your achievements or even dropping a name or two when it's relevant to the conversation, but this constant barrage of "look at me" statements reveals their selfishness or insecurity.

Red flag #9. They don't respect your time or anyone else's. When they schedule an hour consultation with an expert, they try to push it to ninety minutes. When you meet for lunch, they're consistently half an hour late. They get angry when the doctor is ten minutes late for an appointment, but they have no problem arriving late to pick up their kids from school. They're a walking example of the "world revolves around you" cliché.

Red flag #10. They find opportunities to belittle or demean you. Often, they do this under the guise of joking or teasing, but you don't have that kind of relationship and those shots are meant to wound you. This person may want to bring you down to their level or make you feel lucky they would be your friend. Either way, this isn't someone you want in your life or on your team.

Of course, this isn't an exhaustive list of red flags. In choosing your friendships, business relationships, and romantic partners, use your discernment. Follow your intuition, and if you feel like something's not quite right, pay attention to that feeling. When people who care about you share their opinion of this person, be willing to listen. Pray to God for a clear view of who this person really is and what role, if any, they should have in your life.

You will never be bigger than your associations. This can be a hard truth to accept, but it's the way the world works. If you want to be righteous, you must put yourself in spaces with people who strive to live a righteous life. If you want a strong marriage, hang around friends who respect their spouse and are committed to their marriage. If you want to succeed in business, spend time with people who are successful in their own business and doing it the right way. If you want to be a better parent, spend time with friends who are committed to raising their children well. Learn from people who've accomplished what you want for your own life.

As the leader of your life, you have a responsibility to choose with intention the people who get to come into your inner circles. Don't settle for relationships with people who demonstrate questionable character because you think you need them in your network. When God gets ready to birth your future, he'll birth the relationships you need to get there.

MANAGE PEOPLE WITH BOUNDARIES AND GRACE

When I bring new employees into my law firm, I'm always looking to create a three-way win—a win for the new team member, a win for my clients, and a win for my firm. I'm often willing to take a chance on people who don't have years of experience but can demonstrate that they have the smarts, the work ethic, and the desire to learn on the job with training and mentorship from me. Of course, bringing on new people comes with risk. Things don't always go perfectly, even when they're intelligent and capable.

Because I make all the hiring decisions for my firm, I own the results even when a team member doesn't work out. When it works out well, I get to enjoy the expansion of my business, and I get the satisfaction of knowing I'm contributing to someone's career growth. When it doesn't, my bottom line is negatively affected, and I have to deal with any issues. Sometimes, this means providing additional training, and sometimes, it means letting someone go. I never enjoy terminating a team member's employment, but as the leader of my firm, it's a responsibility that falls on me.

Whether you're running your own company, managing a department in your job, supervising a project at your church, or leading your family, you'll often have direct responsibility for managing people. To manage them successfully, I encourage you to do two things: (1) set boundaries and (2) give grace.

By sharing clear expectations with my team members, I set boundaries around the behavior I will and will not accept in my business. I can only hold my team members accountable to those expectations if I've clearly communicated them. That's part of my job as the leader of my firm. The reality, however, is that people do fall short. I don't fire a team member every time he or she gets something wrong. I have processes in place to help them get back on track, develop, and grow in their position. Those processes allow me to give grace to people when they need it. There are also times when grace has been given, but the behavior doesn't change. That's when I may have to enforce my boundaries with a disciplinary process.

Boundaries and grace are as important in your personal relationships as they are in your professional relationships. Set boundaries to let people know what you expect of them. Give them grace when they fail. And enforce your boundaries by changing or ending relationships when you need to do so.

SEEK THE SAME VALUES

Before I met Lauren, I dated a few women who seemed to check all the boxes for what I was looking for in a wife. I later realized that while they met some of the superficial criteria, they weren't made for me. Over time, as they revealed their true nature, not just the face they put on when they wanted to impress me, I discovered our values weren't in alignment at all. In one case, the woman who supposedly wanted to be in a relationship with me constantly put me down. Instead of encouraging me to maximize my potential, she did her best to suppress it. She called me dumb to my face and tried to make me feel inadequate as a person. She treated me as if the way God created me wasn't as special as the way God created her. Fortunately, the relationship didn't last long, but it did some damage.

When I found Lauren, I found a woman who valued me for who I was when we met. She had a desire to help me make the most of the potential I'd barely begun to tap into at that time, and I wanted to do the same for her. Not only did we share the same values, but we also had strengths to balance each other's weaknesses. In my wife, I found someone willing to listen and give me honest feedback, a woman who's always looking out for my best interest.

Leaders can often feel alone in the world. When things don't go as planned, all the blame gets heaped on them. When they face setbacks, some of the people who claim to support them quietly disappear. Sometimes, the people who were the leader's most vocal supporters turn out to have nefarious motives. Challenges like these come with the territory, but the right life partner can make it so much easier to overcome them. Having a partner who's in your corner no matter what life brings is invaluable.

Obviously, most of us want a shared physical attraction with our spouse. But that physical attraction can be found in a lot of places with a lot of people who won't value your other qualities. When you're ready to get serious about a relationship, get serious about character. Assess any potential life partner based on his or her character. Look for core qualities that line up with who the Word of God calls us to be. Study love as it's defined in 1 Corinthians 13, and make sure your relationship can embody this kind of love. Use the Word as your foundation, and then look at your own core values and how they're reflected in the way you live and how you treat people. Make sure your lifestyle and your partners are value aligned.

Lastly, look for the indispensable element in anyone you're considering as a partner. Leaders need leaders in their lives. If you're thinking of marrying a man who can't lead himself in making good decisions, you might want to reconsider. You don't want to end up with a spouse who constantly creates problems you have to solve. If the woman you're thinking of proposing to lacks many of the leadership skills discussed here, slow down. Maybe she's not the one for you, or maybe she's not ready for marriage yet.

Don't marry potential or settle for someone who wants to marry you for who you might one day become. You and your partner should appreciate and desire each other for who you are right now. Work together to maximize your potential as individuals, as a couple, and as a family. What you create with the right partner will be greater than anything you could ever create alone.

BE A GIVER

In the 1990s, my parents had a vision for serving the children in our area who needed it most. They brought their vision to life when they launched a child development center in a low-income neighborhood. They wanted to play a role in helping transform the lives of young Black boys and girls, and they did. As I write this, the center still operates, giving children a safe, structured, and loving place to be while their parents work.

From the beginning, many of the young boys came into the child development center and acted out. Their behavior was clearly a demand for more attention, so I tried to figure out ways to give them attention in a positive manner. Finally, I decided to create a program that would allow some of them to receive male mentorship. Many of these young boys had absent fathers, and I wanted to do what I could to give them a positive model of a Black man.

I took the boys bowling and skating, to visit museums, and out for pizza. We spent whole Saturdays together. I wanted them to have a chance to experience new things but also to receive the time and attention they craved. Most of the mothers appreciated the effort I made. A few, however, quickly began to resent the influence I had on their child. They didn't think it was a bad influence; they just worried it might be too great.

Only in my twenties at the time, I was somewhat naive in my expectations. I didn't expect any pushback or complaints. Why, I wondered, would anyone complain about someone pouring into their child? My time with the boys benefited everyone involved, including the mothers, so I expected everyone to be happy about it. When that turned out not to be the case, I was surprised, but I persevered. Any mother who didn't want her son involved could pull him out, but I continued to show up for those who wanted the mentorship and whose mothers saw the value in it.

Part of being a leader is self-sacrifice. A leader can't be stingy or selfish. Self-centered thinking destroys leadership potential. Remember: Leadership always serves the greater good. It's difficult to positively impact others if you only focus on yourself. The purpose of leadership is to add value.

The sacrifice leadership often requires can feel daunting, especially when it seems like no one notices or cares about your contribution. In Mark 6:4 (KJV), Jesus says, "A prophet is not without honour, but in his own country, and among his own kin, and in his own house." A prophet is without honor in his own land. Sometimes, the people who have the hardest time recognizing your value will be those closest to you, including those you're trying to serve. That doesn't mean you stop giving. Find new ways to serve where your gifts are welcome.

Givers share their time, talents, and money. Many people believe they can't give yet because they don't have a lot of money. They tell themselves they'll tithe at church, donate to the nonprofit they admire, or help a friend in need once they're earning a little more money. But nothing could be more untrue. Giving is a condition of the heart. If you don't give back when you only have a little, you won't give back when you have a lot. You're lying to yourself when you say you will. Start where you are, and give what you can. Part of being a good steward of your money is sharing it in ways that will benefit others.

At the other end of the spectrum, we find people who believe writing big checks is sufficient. However, as a leader, contributions of your time, talent, wisdom, and knowledge can sometimes make an even bigger difference. The money I spent on pizza didn't do nearly as much for those young boys as the time I invested in talking with them did. Mentoring, volunteering on the front lines of a movement, sitting on a board, writing grant proposals for organizations that need funding—these are all ways you can exercise your giving muscle.

Jesus told the rich ruler, who believed himself righteous because he followed the laws and commandments, that if he really wanted to be good, he should sell all he had and follow Jesus. But the ruler didn't love God more than his possessions, and he went away in sorrow. God doesn't need anything you have to offer. He wants your sacrifice as a demonstration of what's in your heart. God wants you to give for the right reasons. Your desire to add value and your recognition that your success is meant to be shared will not only bless others but will also benefit you at the same time. As you ensure others do well alongside you or coming up behind you, you'll be blessed with a life of true contentment and satisfaction. Success without a successor is failure. In your giving, you create a legacy of givers.

When you see a need, do what you can to fill it. When you call out people who need to do better, offer to help them do better. The essence of earthly purpose is to have a positive impact on someone else's life. Use what you've been given to transform someone else. Let your light shine on other people. Then, you'll see the image and glory of God reflected in you.

INDISPENSABLE ACTION STEPS
PEOPLE

Assess your relationships and your heart for giving. Answer the following questions in a journal or document, and use your answers to create an action plan.

1. Are there relationships you need to nurture more? If so, which?
2. Are there people you should spend less time with due to a conflict in values?
3. What new boundaries will you set, and who will you give more grace?
4. Are you happy with your level of giving?
5. How and where will you give more?

DISCERNMENT

Where there is no guidance,
a people falls, but in an abundance of counselors there is safety.
Proverbs 11:14, ESV

WHEN THE PASTOR of a large and active church offered to mentor me in my calling and show me the way, I was flattered. I recognized that it was a sacrifice for him to take time out of his busy schedule to offer me guidance, and I appreciated his willingness to pour into me. I had only recently accepted the call to become a pastor, so the idea of a seasoned and respected mentor in that field appealed to me. Eager to learn and grow, I accepted his offer, and we got to work. Each day, we started with a 5 a.m. devotional, during which we studied the Word, and prayed together. After a few months of working together, he invited me to speak at his church, and I accepted the invitation.

During our time working together, the pastor asked me to sit down with his staff to discuss how they could retain new converts with a follow-up ministry. I had extensive experience with a similar project, and I gladly met with his team and shared my ideas. The pastor also confided in me that one of his challenges was getting people to respond to his altar call. Every pastor has strengths and weaknesses, and by his own estimation, the altar call was a growth opportunity for him. I saw these demonstrations of his trust in me as evidence that we were building a strong foundation for our mentor-mentee relationship, and I felt we'd gotten close through our near-daily interactions. The invitation to preach at his church was an extension of that trust and, from my perspective, strengthened our bond.

Early on the morning that I served as his guest preacher, Lauren and I met with the pastor in his office, and the three of us prayed together. That day, I preached to more than one thousand souls in his congregation, and God used me in a great way. The message that came through me resonated with so many people, and when the pastor got up and made an altar call, many of those folks leaped from their seats and poured down the aisles to the altar. It was a victory for God, and I was humbled by the role I'd played in it. I felt a certain sense of satisfaction but also a desire to get feedback from my mentor. I trusted his experience and I was anxious to know where he believed I could improve.

When we got back to the pastor's office after the service, he was much quieter than usual. I gave him the opportunity to assess my message and the way I delivered it, but he didn't have much to say, and my sense of satisfaction slowly evaporated. Maybe, I thought, I hadn't done very well at all. For the rest of the day, I reflected on my sermon and tried to evaluate how I'd done. From all appearances, people had really responded to the message I'd delivered. Even though I'd seen and heard their positive reactions with my own eyes and ears, I began judging myself and beating myself up for what I might have done better. While my mentor didn't have any specific criticisms for me, he also didn't offer me any positive feedback. He seemed to completely shut down, so I didn't know what to think.

It was important to me to get my mentor's feedback. We'd come together as mentor and mentee for the purpose of improving my preaching skills, and I was committed to that goal. I looked forward to talking with my mentor the next day in our regular morning session, and I waited by my phone at our usual time. When the call didn't come, I rationalized and came up with excuses for him. Surely, he must've gotten busy. On Tuesday, and then Wednesday and Thursday, I again waited, but he never called.

Over the next few weeks, I texted the pastor, but he responded with brief messages or not at all. Finally, I called him to see if everything was OK. "I've just been busy," he explained. But he'd also been busy when he first offered to mentor me. He'd been busy throughout the course of our work together. He led a busy life; however, a packed schedule shouldn't have kept him from communicating with me. If I'd done something wrong in his eyes, I wanted to know so I could correct it and repair the relationship, but he insisted the only thing in the way of our work was his schedule.

After a while, I stopped reaching out to him, and he didn't reach out to me either. I still wondered if I'd inadvertently done something to offend him, but given our relationship, I would've expected him to address any perceived offense with me directly. Whatever the cause, his change in attitude really hurt me. Without any communication from him, I had to draw my own conclusions. I suspected something in the way I showed up for his church had left him feeling insecure. My best guess was the great response to that day's altar call—an area in which he admittedly struggled—left him disturbed or angry with me.

The way our relationship ended disappointed me, but it also reminded me of the importance of discernment. Perhaps I should have gotten to know the pastor better before agreeing to be mentored by him. Perhaps I should have taken more time to pray about it and seriously considered the opportunity before saying yes. Perhaps I should've politely declined his invitation to preach at his church.

I believe he's a good pastor and he leads a good church, but with a little more discernment, I might have avoided the entire situation.

Discernment—your ability to make good decisions based on your judgment of what's right for you and for the people you lead and influence—is essential to your ability to lead in every area of your life. However, this skill comes with maturity and practice. Great leaders develop their discernment over time, but it doesn't happen without effort.

True discernment requires you to assess your choices based on what's right for everyone involved and the season you're in at that time. Often, a new direction may be the right one, but you may be in the wrong season to follow that new path. A great leader weighs both factors before reaching a decision.

DON'T MAKE DECISIONS TOO HASTILY

My first job as an attorney was as a public defender, and for my first few months in the public defender's office, I was enthusiastic about my role. I quickly developed a game plan to close more cases than any of my colleagues, and it worked. Soon, I was contributing at the highest level, working hard to make our part of the system function well. Unfortunately, I didn't get paid based on my contribution. The salary was locked in. I would earn $32,000 a year plus benefits whether I showed up in excellence or mediocrity. My employer didn't dole out bonuses for doing the job exceptionally well.

As a new hire, I had enough sense not to make demands before demonstrating my value, but after I'd been on the job for a year, I also had enough wisdom to compile a report detailing the results I was getting. I planned to present this evidence of my performance when I asked for a raise. With my data in hand, I picked up the phone to schedule a meeting with my boss, but he saw right through my plan. "If you're asking for more money," he said, "I ain't got none, so I can answer that question for you now." And without further discussion, he hung up the phone.

I went home that day and thought about where my career was and where it was headed. At the time, I consistently closed more cases than anybody else on our team. I even underbilled so the department could save money. Day after day, I gave my clients 100 percent, even though they often disrespected me. Despite all that, my boss couldn't be bothered to show me basic consideration. He couldn't make time to sit down and have a face-to-face conversation with me. When I returned to the office, I took my degrees down from the wall and went to work on my exit plan.

During that time, I'd been helping an attorney's assistant at the courthouse on a regular basis. The next time she approached me in court and asked for my assistance with another task, I saw an opportunity. "Your boss has me working so much he might as well just hire me," I told her. Shortly thereafter, she spoke with her boss, who owned his own law firm, and within a few weeks, her boss reached out to offer me a chance to join his team. I asked for nearly twice the salary the public defender's office paid me, and he agreed.

When I resigned from the public defender's office, my supervisor advised me to take most of my cases with me and bill them privately so the department wouldn't have to go through the trouble of reassigning them. This allowed me to enter private practice with more than fifty clients, so I was immediately a profitable hire for my new employer.

I worked for the firm for five years before I decided to go out on my own and launch Huggins Law Firm. Before I left, my boss pitched an offer to me to purchase his law firm as a franchise. It sounded like a less risky way to start my own venture, so I wrote up an agreement and prepared to go through with the deal. Then, he revealed several factors I hadn't considered. He wanted me to pay a franchise fee, cover all the employees' salaries, and pay all utilities for that office. On top of all that, he would require me to give him a percentage of gross, not net, sales. That meant he would take his cut before I paid the first business expense.

Rather than hesitate and take the time to fully examine his offer, I thought about all the money I had made for his firm. I thought of all the money his firm brought in every month, and even though the fees seemed excessive, I figured the business would still do well. I don't mind working hard, and I convinced myself I'd make so much money those additional expenses wouldn't hurt me in the long run. I didn't ask to review the business's tax statements. I didn't ask to see the balance sheets, cash flow statements, accounts receivable, or accounts payable. I'd never bought a business of any kind before that opportunity, and I had no idea that I needed to review those documents to make a good decision.

I saw a thriving business earning good money, and owning it seemed like a great opportunity to get a running start on my new role as an entrepreneur and to accelerate my ability to create a financial legacy for my family. Even with all those red flags waving in my face, I signed the agreement. Worse, I signed it without discussing it with any trusted advisors. Worst of all, I signed it without talking to Lauren.

That night, I came home in a mood to celebrate. "We'll never be broke now," I told Lauren, and I explained the deal. My wife heard me out, and then she said, "But we didn't even talk about it." She was right, but I assured her we had nothing to worry about.

When I told Lauren not to worry, I was confident the deal would be a profitable one, and on that point, I was right. The deal was profitable. But not for me and not for us. After paying payroll, utilities, the $2,500 monthly franchising fee, and 15 percent of gross sales, I had nothing left to take home. It was an incredibly stressful time as money just seemed to fly out the door. In addition, the former owner's staff was still loyal to him, and he was having them do work for him while they were on my payroll. He was still running his business, but now, he was using my resources. The only thing that had changed was that the burden of sustaining the business had shifted to me.

After turning over a portion of my contingency fee from a large settlement I'd won for a client—the biggest I'd brought in at that point in my career—to my former boss, I knew something had to find a way to pivot. I could do bad all by myself. I didn't need a franchisor keeping me broke while I worked long hours every day.

I went to him and explained that our deal wasn't working for me. I told him in no uncertain terms that I wanted out. He relented enough to make a few adjustments in my favor to our arrangement, changes he could've made earlier, but he didn't want to let me out of our contract. Instead, he reminded me I still had a noncompete and couldn't start a firm within twenty-five miles of where we'd been in business together. He made it clear he was serious about enforcing that restriction.

Even though I had to start my new business in a different city, I left the franchise relationship behind and went out on my own. I ran the firm by myself for the first year. Legal intakes, consultations, court appearances, taking calls, updating the calendar—it was a lot, and I did it all. But finally, I was making some money.

Accepting the terms of the franchising agreement without taking time to thoroughly think them through was the worst business decision I ever made. In my haste, I skipped two crucial steps in the decision-making process. First, I failed to get clarity on the facts and the numbers. When some of the numbers didn't appear to be in my favor, I rationalized that I could make them work. Great leaders have to face the facts as they appear in black and white.

As a leader, you cannot allow pride, excitement, or personal desires to outweigh the facts. You're responsible first for yourself, and even if you don't already have a team, a family, or followers, as a leader, you'll eventually have people depending on you too. My wife and family depend on me to make good decisions. My choices affect them. As a business owner, my team members rely on me to run the business effectively and earn a profit. I can't live up to my responsibility in any of those relationships if I choose to ignore the facts.

Practicing discernment doesn't mean you have to make all your decisions on your own. Great leaders know when to consult with someone else—the second step I skipped. They know where to seek advice, or they're willing to do the work to find the right person to advise them. Always consult with your spouse before you make a major business or life decision. If you're in a healthy relationship, then your spouse has your best interests at heart. He or she will look for any possible downsides of a decision because they desire to protect you. Often, your spouse will have more distance from the decision and can see something in the equation that you're overlooking. Keep in mind also that your marriage is a partnership and any decision you make will affect both of you. Give your spouse room to be heard before you make important choices.

In addition to discussing the decision with Lauren, I should've sought wise counsel from someone who'd successfully done what I wanted to do. It's fine to discuss your moves with your friends and family members, but for the most part, unless they've been where you're trying to go, they can't be your sole source of advice. Never go to anybody for specific advice unless they have a proven track record of success in that area. It might have taken me some time and effort to find the right person to advise me, but I could've avoided a lot of headaches if I'd bothered to find a wise advisor.

The Bible says in the multitude of counsellors, there is safety (Proverbs 11:14), but my excitement and enthusiasm got the best of me in this case. I looked at the potential to earn a lot of money, and I made a hasty decision without seeking advice from people who knew more than I did about buying a business. Even input from someone who didn't know a lot about business but who was neutral on the issue could have saved me a lot of time and lost money. And of course, my wife deserved to have input in a decision of this magnitude, which affected our family finances and how much time I had to spend at home.

Finally, a great leader always goes to the ultimate source of wisdom before making an important decision. In my haste to move to the next level of my career and become a business owner, I didn't spend enough time in prayer, seeking God's counsel about this decision. Instead, I tried to lean on my own understanding, and I paid a price for it. There's always wisdom to be found in God's word and in seeking his guidance through prayer.

PICK YOUR BATTLES

As a leader, you'll find there's always a new battle you could fight. A coworker fails to do their part on a project and sets you up to take the blame. Your boss interrogates you and tries to make you feel guilty when you take time off to spend with your sick child. A repeat customer gives you a lot of business but constantly makes late payments, causing you to struggle to make payroll. Your state government passes a new law making it difficult for marginalized citizens to vote and jeopardizing this country's promise of free and fair elections. On the way to work, someone cuts you off on the freeway. Your spouse forgets to pay a bill, and you're hit with a huge, totally avoidable fee. The list of daily annoyances, challenges, and potential conflicts can seem to have no end.

Every day, events occur that have the potential to negatively impact you and the people you lead. However, you only have the bandwidth—your available time and mental and emotional energy—to deal with a select few of those events. You have to choose which are important enough for you to take on. Early in your development as a leader, it can be tempting to run head-on into every challenge, just to prove you can or because you feel responsible for so many people. But as you mature and develop discernment, you realize some battles aren't worth fighting.

To decide if a battle is worth fighting, ask yourself the following questions.

1. Who is my opponent?
2. How formidable is my opponent?
3. Am I equipped to win this battle right now?
4. What would be the cost of winning this battle?
5. What would be the reward for winning this battle?

Before you can decide if a battle is worth fighting, you must know your opponent. Anyone trying to stop you from fulfilling the destiny God has called you to fulfill is your opponent. Anything less serious than that is usually not a battle you need to fight. Based on that definition, the person who cut you off in traffic on your morning commute and the cashier with the smart mouth probably aren't your opponents. They may be annoying, but if they're not standing between you and your purpose in any material way, engaging with them is probably a waste of your time and energy.

Once you recognize your opponent, evaluate their strengths and weaknesses to the best of your ability. After you assess your opponent, consider your own readiness for battle. How do your strengths and weaknesses compare to theirs? Where might you need help to win this battle? Although the fight may seem like an important one, the timing may not be right for you to take it on. If you decide it is, before you jump in, make sure you have the necessary resources and support to win the battle. Be willing to call in reinforcements when you need help.

Regardless of how well prepared you may be, every battle has a cost. Assessing the cost requires you to stop and think about what you're pursuing and why. Be honest with yourself about what you'll have to sacrifice. Be honest, also, about your motivation and intention. If you're trying to become a rapper, for example, is your motivation all about money? Are you out to change the world in a positive way with your lyrics, or are you looking to get rich at any cost?

As you examine your reasons for taking on any battle, keep in mind that the Bible tells us the love of money is the root of all evil (1 Timothy 6:10). When the accumulation of money *for your own sake* is your goal, you're likely to do almost anything, at any cost, to fight the battles you believe you need to fight. People who love money often make sacrifices they later regret. They sacrifice their marriage, relationships with their children, their well-being, and their values. A battle that could cost you those things is probably not worth fighting.

Lastly, get clear about the potential rewards of any battle you choose to fight. Only you can decide if they're enough to make the battle worthwhile. Doing what God has called you to do, using your gifts to glorify God, the satisfaction of completing a personal goal, leaving a legacy for the next generation, having a positive impact on the people who follow you or even on people who will never know your name—these are rewards great leaders choose to fight for because they're worth winning.

You cannot fight every battle that comes your way. Your time on this earth and your other resources are all finite. Don't waste them on battles that, at best, will leave you with a hollow victory. Pick your battles wisely.

KNOW WHAT YOU WANT AND ASK FOR IT

Knowing what you want and asking for it doesn't mean you'll always get it. I knew what I wanted from my job at the public defender's office—a higher salary. I had worked hard for it. I had earned it, and I was prepared to ask for it. However, my employers weren't willing to give it to me. In that case, my best alternative was to move on and find what I wanted elsewhere. You won't always get what you ask for in the moment, but if you don't ask, you're much less likely to receive.

In any relationship, from your marriage and parent-child relationships to your relationships with your clients and customers or your employer, it's crucial to know what you want and to speak up about it when appropriate. Nowhere is this more important than in your family relationships. Many marriages could be saved if more of us mastered the art of understanding what we want and communicating it *before* we walked down the aisle. All too often, couples marry without first confirming that they're seeking the same things from marriage. This leads to unnecessary conflicts over everything from finances to parenting styles. Practice discernment in choosing what you ask for in your relationships, but ask.

You also have to apply discernment in getting to know yourself and what you want from your life. Too many people are in jobs that make them miserable only because they can't think of something better to do. In any position, you have the opportunity to maximize the moment by building your skills and growing your character, but if you stay in that position for too long because you don't know where you want to go, you'll eventually struggle to find contentment. God puts us in situations for a season so we can grow; however, it's up to us to discern when that season is over. My first job as a teenager was at Winn-Dixie. I enjoyed the job. I was good at it. I developed skills there that still serve me today. Working at Winn-Dixie served me well when I was fifteen years old, but if I was still working there, I doubt if I'd be happy. Instead, I asked myself what I wanted and committed to going after it.

Effective leaders develop the clarity to identify what they want through prayer, study, observation, and seeking wise counsel. They can articulate it clearly and persuasively. They also know how to respond when they get what they want and when they don't. If you lack clarity about what you want from a relationship, you'll end up frustrated because your spouse will have a hard time guessing what you need. When you lack clarity on your assignment and purpose, when you don't know what you're called or gifted to do, that confusion can lead to dissatisfaction. You'll often end up unhappy and dissatisfied with what you're doing because you're not operating in your gifts or calling. If you're called to be a professor but you're working in a hospital, that's going to lead to frustration—unless that work is a part of your purpose.

When you know what you want, on the other hand, and can effectively communicate it and pursue it, you greatly increase your chances of getting it. People who love and care about you will go out of their way to help you achieve your goals and fulfill your desires. The leadership in your life, such as your supervisor or boss, will consider your desires when making decisions that affect you. Your followers will do what they can to make it easier for you to achieve what you've set out to do. When you know what you want in any area of your life, and you tell more of the right people what that is, you're much more likely to find someone who can help you get it.

INDISPENSABLE ACTION STEPS
DISCERNMENT

Choose one area of your life where you feel frustrated or stuck. Take a few minutes to write a list of what you want in that area. (Remember not to focus on what you *don't* want. Write your goals and desires.) Then, pick one goal to pursue right now. Answer the following questions about that goal.

1. What exactly do I want?
2. Is this the right time for me to pursue this goal? (If not, choose another goal.)
3. Why do I want this goal?
4. Who do I need to discuss my pursuit of this goal with before I begin? (Consider who will be affected and who can provide you with wise counsel.)

Finally, take the first step by having an open conversation with someone on your list. You're free to choose anyone you think can give you good advice or who will be impacted by your decisions, but stay open-minded and seriously consider their input.

FAITH

*Let us not become weary in doing good, for at the proper
time we will reap a harvest if we do not give up.*
Galatians 6:9, NIV

PEOPLE OFTEN LOOK at a happily married pastor and first
lady, like my wife and me, and think they must have enjoyed
a perfect relationship from day one. They imagine we never
argue or disappoint each other in any way. However, pastors and first
ladies are still men and women. We experience ups and downs in our
relationships too. In fact, when Lauren and I were dating, we went
through a painful breakup. We might never have seen each other
again, but we still attended the same church, where we were both
actively involved, so we crossed paths at least once a week. For me,
the constant reminder of how things had gone wrong between us only
kept the wound open longer.

I found it difficult to get over the way things ended between us.
Every Sunday, I strolled into church eager to learn the Word but
also holding unforgiveness and bitterness in my heart toward her.
For months, I lifted my hands to praise God, and at the same time,
I wanted her to regret losing me. In truth, I wanted her to want me

back even though I told myself it was over. I looked all good on the outside. I showed up as I always had and did the right things, but inside, I held on to resentment. Even when I read the Word of God or heard it preached, it didn't change my feelings on this one issue. The Word couldn't transform my heart or renew my mind in relationship to Lauren because my heart and mind were closed to it. My negative feelings for her had started to slow my growth in my faith.

Harboring bad feelings around the relationship never felt right to me, and with time, it only felt more misaligned with the man I wanted to be. Something needed to change in me, and one day, I felt compelled to give God a supernatural forgiveness offering. It was distressingly clear that I couldn't forgive Lauren on my own strength. Holding on to the breakup was holding me back in my faith walk, which affected every area of my life. I was still growing in my faith, but not the way I wanted to, and I decided to give God a $1,000 forgiveness offering. (If you're wondering, please know this was a significant amount of money for me.) I prayed for God to uncover grace and compassion in my heart, and I believe prayer works, but the offering was my way of also releasing my faith. It was my way of giving God something sacrificial to work with in healing my heart.

God answered my prayers—and not by changing Lauren. He didn't cause her to seek me out or apologize to me. He didn't inspire her to move to another church so we wouldn't have to look at each other anymore. Instead, he answered my prayers by changing me. In the beginning, I wanted her to see me shine so she'd feel bad about letting me go. I wanted her to see she'd made a mistake and wish she could have me back, but God said, "No, you need to start praying *for her.*" I resisted the idea, but in the end, I chose to be obedient, and I began to pray for Lauren every day.

Taking the focus off what I wanted her to do and how I wanted her to change opened me up to hear from God and receive his blessings once again. Then one day, when Lauren unexpectedly spoke to me in church, I politely responded. Over the following weeks, we went from a terse "Good morning" and "How are you?" to engaging in conversations. My heart began to change, and I saw her through new eyes. I saw who she really was and how things had gone wrong between us. When I finally asked her out again, she agreed to go.

On that first date, I sat across from Lauren and cried like a baby. We went on three or four dates, and I cried half the time on each of them. Finally, I could see and acknowledge what I'd been missing by being so hardheaded. I loved this woman! God had given me this gift, and I had taken her for granted and almost lost her. Now, God had blessed me with a second chance—and it all started with releasing my faith with that sacrificial seed offering.

There is no success without sacrifice. In order to make an investment in anything, you have to give up something. When you invest in the stock market, you sacrifice some of your hard-earned money in hopes that it will return a harvest to you. When you invest in your career, you sacrifice time you could spend on other pursuits. You sacrifice the money you spend on your professional development with the goal of becoming more of who you were created to be.

Investing in your faith is no different. Find a point of leverage that works for you and take action on it. You may need to make a sacrificial offering to activate your faith. You may need to give more than your usual tithe, or you may need to sacrifice something completely different. Perhaps you need to sacrifice your ego and role-play a conversation with a proxy before stepping out on faith to have a tough conversation. Watching a sermon online or reading a book may also serve to activate your faith. The point is to *take some step* to demonstrate your faith. Move in the direction of what you're asking God to do for you and trust God to move with you.

I've preached so many sermons on faith. It's a subject I love to discuss and one you could study for a lifetime and never fully master. As you might imagine, there are many different definitions of the word.

Faith is seeing the invisible before it's made visible. Faith is trusting in the eventual manifestation of your vision. You have to choose what faith means to you. However, the most important faith practice for leaders is faith in the Word of God, trusting that what the Bible says is as true for you today as it was for the people who lived through that history.

Leadership always involves risks. No matter how risk averse or how willing to gamble you may be, as a leader, you make decisions that affect you and other people. Some decisions will work out in your favor, and some won't. Faith enhances your decision-making ability. Because you trust all things will work for your good in the end (Romans 8:28), just as God has promised, you don't need to make decisions from a position of panic or desperation. Your faith leads you to study the Word of God and grow wiser in the process so you can grow as a believer and as a leader. If a decision doesn't go your way—and sometimes they won't—you have faith that you can learn from it and use that new knowledge and wisdom to pivot or make a better choice in the next situation.

As a believer, growing your faith is a never-ending practice. As a leader, you focus on your faith not just for your own benefit but also for the benefit of others. There will be times when you have to believe not just for yourself but also for your followers when they're weak in faith. As your faith deepens, you'll attract more of the right people who support you in growing your faith. Living in faith causes people to gravitate to you. They can see in you the strength and courage that comes from knowing what God says about you and his plans for you.

KNOW YOUR SOURCE

Your source is the place from which you draw your strength. It's the support system you turn to when you're weak. It's where you go for help when you can't accomplish what you set out to do on your own. As a person of faith, you must recognize and embrace God as your one true source.

The only way to know your source for yourself is to know the Word for yourself. You can't just take someone else's word for what the Bible says about you and your relationship with God. Great leaders seek to understand. You have to read and study the Word for yourself, but you don't have to figure it all out for yourself. Follow mature spiritual leadership and seek solid mentorship in your faith walk. Don't look for perfection in your teachers—you won't find it. Look for someone striving to live a lifestyle in alignment with God's word.

You may also come to know your source through a revelation or personal encounter with God. In that case, you must have knowledge of the truth, which can only be found in God's word. Then, you can apply this knowledge and the leading of the Holy Spirit to know what's real and what's false. Be aware that Satan can conjure falsehoods that could appear to be revelations if you don't know the truth of what God says. Always know that anything that contradicts the Word of God is false. Any "revelation" that contradicts the Word is a lie and a trick, no matter how real it appears, but you can only recognize that deception when you know what the Bible says.

A personal encounter with God will rarely look like a scene from the movies. Very few people see the clouds part and hear a voice from on high. Most of us will never watch a bush burn without being consumed. God doesn't take earthly form to appear in front of most of us, but God speaks to us in many ways. Your personal encounter with God might be as simple as having an epiphany or reaching a new understanding. It might come through a dream or through receiving a new and crucial piece of information or a sudden explosion of knowledge. Listen and verify what you learn from your encounter with God by verifying it through the Word of God.

I had been praying for a wife for some time before Lauren and I connected, and a few women came my way. They looked like candidates, but they were counterfeits. They looked like wife material for me, but time revealed that they weren't. When I had a revelation from God that Lauren was a potential wife for me, I realized how much I had underestimated and failed to appreciate her true worth. Lauren is beautiful on the outside; however, she's also beautiful in deeper ways. She has the qualities of a virtuous woman. If I didn't know God's word, Satan could have deceived me into believing a less suitable woman was the right woman for me to marry. Not only would I have missed out on my life with Lauren and our family, but I could also have experienced a world of hurt in choosing the wrong woman to make my wife.

As a leader, you have a responsibility to the people who follow you. If you claim to believe the Bible, then the truth of scripture can't be open to interpretation based on what you'd like it to say. When you have a relationship with God, he can also take away desires born of the flesh so you can overcome the kinds of temptations that have gotten even great leaders off track, the kind of temptation I almost fell for in my dating life.

When you recognize God as your source, you choose to lead people based on how God's manual for our lives says it should be done. You need to lead truthfully—not based on your personal truth but grounded in the unchanging truth of the Word of God. Lead in authenticity and honesty. Be open with how you assess yourself, where you are in life, and in what areas you still need to grow. Through it all, keep in mind and make clear to your followers that your plans and choices are in alignment with concrete truths and convictions.

PRACTICE OBEDIENCE

Knowing your source through consistent study of the Bible and the guidance of strong mentors prepares you to practice obedience to

God. There's no shortage of self-proclaimed gurus and influencers who offer you their own spiritual philosophies. They compete for your attention and solicit your obedience every day on social media, through their books, and through every media platform from podcasts to movies. They would each have you believe their way is the right way. Many leaders and leaders in the making have fallen victim to these counterfeits and gotten off track with their calling because they failed to practice obedience to their true source. Obedience is essential to any faith practice. It's a demonstration of what you believe to be true.

During the time when Lauren and I were broken up, two fellow Christians told me, "You're going to regret breaking up with her. We believe God brought her into your life." They were correct, but I couldn't receive it yet. Sometimes, you have to see things for yourself to get the lesson. You can't live off someone else's revelation; I had to receive my own revelation and move in obedience to it in order to understand what I was missing by not having Lauren in my life.

I almost lost Lauren because I was seeking what the world told me to seek. Once I had her back, I didn't want to mess it up because I knew I might not get a third opportunity to make the right decision. So on December 25, 2010, in front of her family, who had gathered at her grandparents' house to celebrate Christmas, I proposed to Lauren. God had brought into my life a woman who had all the qualities of a great wife and wonderful mother, and I had the pleasure of demonstrating my obedience to God by marrying her.

Obedience is doing what you were asked to do. It's fulfilling the requirements set forth by an authority figure in your life. As a parent, if I ask my kids to quit jumping on my bed, they can demonstrate obedience by doing what I say. This demonstrates their respect for my role as a primary authority figure in their lives. Obedience to God is just as simple. Do what God asks you to do. Many people will try to convince you that you get to decide what obedience looks like, but in reality, the only way to be submitted to God is to strive to live your life in alignment with what he asks of you.

Your role as a leader does not exempt you from obedience to your Creator. In fact, leadership makes your obedience even more important. Your decisions and your actions have the potential to positively impact or negatively affect everyone who follows you. Holding yourself accountable to the standard set by God's word demonstrates your faith in God.

You will fall short in your faith walk, of course. Your imperfect obedience is part of the human condition. When you contradict the Word of God in thought, word, or deed, your faith requires you to repent, ask for forgiveness, and keep moving forward. Know that this is true of all leaders, including those preaching the Word on Sunday mornings. Too often, society puts leaders—especially pastors—on a pedestal. We build them up until they seem almost mythical. We expect them to be perfect, and when they fail, we come down hard on them, forgetting that God gives us all the opportunity to repent and do better. We all fall short, but we all have a path to forgiveness and the chance to start anew.

Strive for obedience to God as you lead yourself and others. Study God's word and do your best to lead in your own life by following his instructions. When you find yourself straying from God's path, sincerely repent, temporarily step away from leadership if the situation calls for it, and do what's necessary to get back in obedience.

PRAY FOR YOUR ENEMIES

Anyone who tries to achieve greatness and rise above the average will experience resistance. Any leader who has achieved greatness, in ways big or small, has learned to effectively deal with those challenges, especially when that resistance is embodied by people who would do their best to stop that leader from fulfilling their divine destiny. You are not exempt from those challenges. No leader is. When enemies come against you—and they will—it may be tempting to curse them, but great leaders know better. Great leaders bless their enemies.

You may recoil from the thought of opening your mouth to pray for someone who would do you harm, but you likely know God commands us to pray for our enemies. On the surface that sounds like a sacrifice for their sake, but this act will benefit you even more than it benefits the people you're praying for God to bless. Praying for your enemies opens the door to love.

Love is a healing agent, but you can't love people when you're unwilling to pray for them. Prayer is the first step in walking in love toward a person. Prayer allows you to put your enemy's needs before your selfish desires to see them destroyed or dismissed. Praying for your enemies is one of the greatest acts of submitting to God's will.

Praying for the person who has offended you also helps you start and finalize the process of forgiveness. When God told me to start praying for Lauren after our breakup, it was the last thing I wanted to do. But petitioning God on her behalf led me to forgive her, led her to forgive me, and brought us back together. Had I been disobedient and refused to pray for her, there's a good chance we wouldn't be together now. I would've lost out on a wonderful woman because of my pride and bitterness, both of which can kill a relationship and knock you off course in any area of your life.

If you want to stay in the Spirit, don't pray for vengeance or reprisal. To stay biblically correct, pray the Word over your enemies. Leave your desires out of it. Pray that God's will be done in their lives. Your heart will eventually soften enough to allow you to forgive your enemy. Even if you're never reconciled with that person the way I was with Lauren, you will be set free by that forgiveness. Unforgiveness requires you to dwell on the past, and when you're stuck in the past, you can't move forward. Forgiving your enemies releases you from the hurts of the past so you can focus on fulfilling your divine destiny today and in the future.

THE LAW OF FAITH

The Bible says God has dealt to every man (and woman) a measure of faith—not just every Christian or every spiritual person, but *every* person (Romans 12:3). You have the ability to believe that the unseen will be manifested. The decision you must make is whether you trust that God is the source of that manifestation or someone or something else is. Everyone has the gift of faith, but some people put their faith in themselves and their own mental gifts, their physical prowess, or the people they depend on to provide for and take care of them. Others put their faith in their bank account or the stock market. But these people and things are all flawed and imperfect, and placing your faith in them must inevitably lead to disappointment. I choose to put my faith in God and his promises to me. You get to choose where you put yours.

I know how frustrating it can be to watch people who seem to put their faith in *everything but God* prosper while you labor without results. These people don't profess to be Christians. They don't live by God's word, and without those guidelines to live by, they feel free to take all kinds of shortcuts on the road to success. And yet, from all appearances, they reap the benefits of their efforts. Where you struggle, they succeed. Where you take two steps back, they take giant leaps forward. It just doesn't seem fair.

It can be disheartening and confusing to try to do the right thing while watching someone win by doing the wrong thing. What you need to know is that some laws are immutable. These laws always apply even to people who don't place their faith in God. The law of reciprocity, for example, boils down to reaping what you sow. This law applies to everyone, not just to Christians. Keep in mind, however, that you have no idea what anyone is truly reaping. Because you see someone sow chaos and reap financial reward doesn't mean that's all there is to the story. They may be reaping chaos in other areas of their lives, but by law, they will indeed reap it.

When we operate in faith, we receive the promises of God. This is the fulfillment of the law of faith. However, the law of faith doesn't say when or how we'll receive the fulfillment of those promises. It may be controversial to say so, but some people do see a certain kind of success from operating in faith to something or someone other than God. Even if that thought bothers you, it's still the law. However, you should know that anyone who places their faith in something other than God cannot receive the fullness of God's blessings.

While you may see the success of people who misplace their faith, you only see a small part of their lives. You have no idea what may be happening to their relationships or their physical, mental, and spiritual well-being. Just as they're sowing and reaping material gain without the Word of God, they're sowing and reaping discord and disappointment in areas of their lives that matter much more than money. Anyone who fails to sow to the Spirit fails to reap the rewards of the Spirit (Galatians 6:8).

Even when you're unaware of it, the people you lead and influence are always watching you. They pay attention to everything you say and do, and they're aware of where you place your faith. You cannot call yourself a great leader if you're influencing people to place their faith anywhere other than in God.

It takes courage to answer the calling you feel to first lead in your own life and then to lead others. It's much easier to let someone else take the risks, make the difficult decisions, and be held responsible for the results. True leadership requires you to step up as a leader and be willing to grow in that role. It's a step of faith to submit to God and pursue God's will for your life when you may not know where it will take you. Faith in your Heavenly Father and his promises to you allows you to rely on something greater than your own strength, your own bravery, or your own abilities to accomplish your goals.

When I became a pastor, I really had no idea what twists and turns lay on the road ahead. I expected a lot of support, which didn't materialize, but I still had to step into the unknown and follow God's will for my life. That can be scary, but it's also the beautiful part of living by faith. Following God's plan for you is a great adventure. While you may only be able to see the next step, and not the destination, one thing you can count on is that God has plans to prosper you. When you choose to follow him, his plan will lead you into a maximized life like nothing else can.

INDISPENSABLE ACTION STEPS
FAITH

As a leader, it's essential to periodically stop and ask yourself where you're placing your faith and how you're demonstrating that choice. Before moving on from this chapter, take some time to pray about where God wants you to up-level your practice of your faith in him.

Ask yourself the following questions and pray for God's guidance in answering and in taking action on those answers.

1. Do you need to get to know God better?
2. Are there areas of your life where you've fallen into a habit of disobedience? If so, what are they, and where will you start to make a change?
3. Are you holding on to hurts, small or large, from the past? What enemies do you need to pray for so God can release you from that unforgiveness?
4. Do you trust the law of faith, which says that by placing your faith in God, you will receive the fullness of God's blessings? How do you demonstrate this in your daily life? Do your works correspond with your faith? And how can you be an even better model of the law of faith?

CONFESSIONS FOR LEADERS

The law of confession is one of the most powerful spiritual tools you can use to activate your faith. This law tells us you live or die by what you say. You succeed or fail by the words that come out of your mouth. They impact your atti-tude, your health, and your vision. There is power in your words. Activate your faith by making these confessions for leaders a part of your daily life. Write them. Read them. And speak them.

1. I have the indispensable element of leadership in my life.
2. I am a faith-filled, successful leader in competition with no one.
3. I am an integral leader by God's grace.
4. I am a positive leader with vision, adding value to others.
5. I am using my gifts to lead in every area of my life.
6. I lead myself and others in our God-ordained purposes.
7. The best is yet to come for me as a leader.

START WHERE YOU ARE

*Everyone to whom much was given, of him
much will be required, and from him to whom they
entrusted much, they will demand the more.*
Luke 12:48, ESV

YOUR GIFT CAN take you to the top, but only your character will keep you there. It's time to use your talents and skills to make a difference in the world and to create the life you want. Build that success on the values shared here. A commitment to live by godly values separates leaders from people who happen to be in leadership positions. The choice to act with character regardless of the circumstances marks you as a leader even when you have no official title or role. While leading isn't always easy, God has given you everything you need to lead and succeed in the ways he designed you to do. Your life will still have dry seasons and seasons of harvest, but you're always called to be the leader in your own life and wherever you can have the greatest positive impact.

Just as leaders get to enjoy wins and achievements, like everyone else, you'll also deal with betrayal, disappointment, and failure. Sooner or later, every leader has to go through the fire. In fact, you will be tested over and over again. How you respond to those tests determines whether you ultimately fail or succeed. You can do all the right things, for the right reasons and with the right intentions, and still get the wrong results. When this occurs, remember who you are, look for the positive, and take the time to learn something from the situation. When you follow those steps, you can still turn a short-term loss into a long-term win.

You have an incredible future ahead of you, but sometimes, the decisions you make as a leader will be unpopular with your peers, colleagues, followers, or team members. They may react in ways that hurt you. They may try to undermine your decisions or stand in the way of your progress. You can't control other people's behavior, but as a leader, you can always choose how you respond. You can choose to act in alignment with God's word. If you know what the right thing is and you're choosing to do what God would have you do, then you can't be swayed by other people's opinions. Make the best possible decision and have a plan in place to deal with the consequences, good or bad.

God created you to be a leader. He has given you the indispensable element. You need only to tap into it and develop it. You will certainly face challenges and setbacks on that journey, but when you use the Six Keys to Leadership—gifts, vision, integrity, people, discernment, and faith—as your guideposts, you can trust your ability to thrive in spite of those obstacles. Rely on your values, and don't be afraid to make the right decision even when it may cost you time, frustration, or your reputation.

You're embarking on a journey that will transform your life and the lives of the people around you. As you become more successful, more enemies and haters will come out to try to destroy you. Even people you don't know may attack you. Look at Lebron James. So many people hate him without justification. Just read the comments left about him on ESPN articles. Even when he's averaging twenty-five points a game, they want to tear him down.

This need to try to destroy a champion comes from a place of envy and a lack of confidence in their own ability to achieve anything that matters. This kind of backlash isn't reserved for star athletes and celebrities, however. It's directed at anyone who's winning. At some point, that will be you.

When you're in the background, not doing much with your life, people tend to leave you alone, but when you step up to lead, there are always a few people who want to shut you down. With consistent effort, you'll achieve more of your goals, and as you achieve more, you'll become a greater target. Some people see an eagle soar and can't wait to shoot it down. Because they have little going on in their own lives, they can't help but take shots at you. Learn how to fly around those shots and learn how to recover when you're hit by relying on the Six Keys to Leadership.

SET YOUR STANDARD AND STICK TO IT

Make these Six Keys to Leadership the standard for how you live your life.

1. **Gifts:** Recognize your natural, God-given talents and abilities and use them to achieve your goals and God's purpose for your life.
2. **Vision:** See the destination you're striving to reach and the future you imagine.
3. **Integrity:** Do the right thing, at all times, even when no one else will know and even when doing the wrong thing might feel good or benefit you in the moment.
4. **People:** Make careful decisions about the people you surround yourself with and commit to giving back to those in need.

5. **Discernment:** Make good decisions based on your judgment of what's right for you and for the people you lead and influence.

6. **Faith:** See the invisible before it becomes visible. Trust in God and his promises to you.

A NOTE ON YOUR FINANCIAL GOALS

One day, as I waited for a haircut with a new barber, the conversation turned to the Church, and one of the barbers had a lot to say. He didn't come flat out and say the Church is all about taking your money, but he heavily implied it. No one in the shop knew I was a preacher, and for a while I just sat back and listened while everyone laughed. However, the negative talk about the Church kept going on, and I couldn't keep quiet.

Another patron came in and loudly announced, "Man, I missed my gospel this morning."

The barber responded, "You can still give a donation to the church. The church got Cash App and PayPal and every way to pay them!"

"So what's wrong with the Church having Cash App and PayPal?" I asked, my voice raised.

And everybody got quiet.

I waited for the barber to come back at me, but he just shrugged his shoulders. Left unchallenged, he had jokes about the Church, but once he was questioned, he had nothing to say. Sadly, he had only expressed what a lot of people believe. Over the years, the biblical view of money and what it means for a Christian to pursue financial goals has come up in lots of barbershop debates, social media comments, and private conversations. Because a small percentage of pastors have abused their members' trust, many people have the idea that every church just wants your money.

Critics mock building funds and love offerings, but they neglect to consider the expenses involved in maintaining a building, keeping the lights on, and paying people for the time they give to a church. They want churches to make a difference in the community and accomplish great things, but they forget we all operate in an economy that requires cash. It costs money to lead missions, offer youth programs, and provide services and support for members. Growth for any organization or institution requires both human capital and financial capital.

In the same way that many people criticize the Church for having financial goals, some people, especially those who like to consider themselves above money, will denounce you for pursuing monetary success. They often point to 1 Timothy 6:10, which says, "For the love of money is the root of all evil: which while some coveted after, they have erred from the faith, and pierced themselves through with many sorrows." I love addressing this verse because it's one of the most often quoted and one of the most misunderstood.

Notice the verse doesn't say *money* is evil. It says *the love of money* is the root of all evil. Money is neutral. How you think of it and how you use it will determine whether it's a blessing or a curse in your life. Just like money is a tool for the Church to do good in the world, it's a tool for you to achieve goals like safety, security, and opportunity for you and your family. Money is a tool God can use to bless you. Is it evil to have the money to pay your bills and keep your heat on in your house in the middle of winter? Is it evil to be able to put gas in your car and buy new tires when you need them? Is it evil to be able to afford to travel and see more of God's creation?

God has been making his people rich since the beginning of time. Abraham, Job, David, and King Solomon are just a few of the men we see blessed with riches in the Bible. In modern times, the idea of money as evil has been used to oppress poor people and keep them in poverty. The enemy doesn't want believers to amass wealth because he knows true Bible-believing Christians can do a lot of damage to darkness and do a lot of good when they have the money to back up their desire to serve God. Satan knows a Christian who has a successful business will tithe, donate to nonprofit organizations, bless someone with a home or a car, or pay for a college student's tuition. Anyone living by God's instruction to us will find as many ways as possible to use that money for good.

Whenever someone quotes a Bible verse to you as evidence that God wants you to be poor, you need to do deeper research and understand the true meaning and context of that verse. As you set and pursue your goals as a leader, don't be afraid to set bold goals for your financial freedom and the ability to bless others with your financial success. The pursuit of prosperity only becomes a problem when it separates you from God or from the people you're called to love and serve.

As a leader, you will define success for yourself. For most people, this includes some combination of a strong and happy family, a healthy relationship, career advancement, physical health, and financial freedom. My definition of success is much simpler and can encompass all these desires and more. True success consists of building a strong relationship with God while fulfilling your God-ordained purpose in life. It doesn't matter what your purpose is on this earth. It makes no difference how you're called to use your gifts and maximize your life or who you're called to serve and lead. Your deeper purpose remains, now and until you breathe your last breath, to give glory to God in all you do, becoming more Christlike in the process.

INDISPENSABLE ACTION STEPS

Start where you are. Don't wait to get a promotion, finish your degree, or launch your business. Don't wait for someone to anoint you the leader. Step up as the leader in your own life and a leader in your circles of influence starting today.

Follow these steps to apply what you've learned in *The Indispensable Element*:

Step #1. If you've skipped parts of this book or the exercises, go back. Leaders don't skip steps, and they don't seek short-cuts. Read through all the chapters, especially any chapters where you think you already have that leadership key on lock. Pay the price to get the knowledge you need. Leaders pursue a lifetime of growth.

Step #2. Decide to start fresh from today. Whatever you've done or not done so far in your life, whatever has happened to you up to now, you can put the past behind you. Stand on your accomplishments and learn from your failures. Don't be discouraged if it feels like you have a long way to go to create the life you dream of living. We all get there one day at a time.

Step #3. Compare yourself only to who you were yesterday. It's great to have mentors and people you look up to, and sometimes, walking in their footsteps can help you get to your destination faster. However, comparing your progress to anyone else's is a mistake. Don't aspire to be the next

Bishop T. D. Jakes or the next Oprah Winfrey. Aspire to be the best version of you. Be careful, also, not to get caught up in the erroneous belief that a mentor's job is to make you greater than they are. In reality, a mentor's role in your life is only to guide and support you to become as great as God has called you to be.

Step #4. Choose one of the Six Keys to Leadership to focus on over the next thirty days. Read that chapter again and review your responses to the exercises. Keep track of the changes you see in your life as you focus on this one area. Choose a new leadership key to focus on each month and take note of the difference it makes in the way you live your life.

Step #5. Scan the QR code to connect with me and access free resources I've created to support you as you develop your leadership skills to the next level.

MY PRAYER FOR YOU

Father, I pray for every person reading this book will receive your grace to activate the Six Keys for Indispensable Leadership in order to connect with their God-ordained purpose and become agents of change.

I pray every reader knows everything that has happened in their life, good or bad, God will use it for good.

Lord, raise up an army of strong, enduring leaders across the globe, who won't stop at signs of resistance but will push through the pain and every obstacle they may face.

God, enlarge their vision and capacity as leaders and bless them to fulfill their calling and purpose in you.

Lord, I pray leaders are encouraged, inspired, and empowered by this book to go back to their organizations, families, and communities and lead with confidence and excellence.

As a result of being the leaders you have called them to be, may they impact the world and hear from you, "Well done!"

In Jesus' Name, Amen.

ABOUT THE AUTHOR

Micah E. Huggins is a dynamic leader, motivational speaker, and community leader with a passion for helping others discover and develop their leadership abilities. He firmly believes everyone has the innate ability to lead and anyone can step up and fulfill their potential with the right guidance and motivation.

Micah is an accomplished attorney, holding a law degree from the prestigious University of North Carolina School of Law and a Bachelor of Arts in Political Science from the University of North Carolina at Greensboro. As an attorney, he has been honored with numerous awards for his outstanding work in the field. The National Academy of Criminal Defense has recognized him as one of the "Top 10 Attorneys under 40" from the state of North Carolina, and he has also been recognized as one of the top three criminal defense lawyers in Greensboro.

Micah's unwavering dedication to helping others unlock their full potential sets him apart as an attorney and as a pastor. He has devoted countless hours to pastoring and speaking engagements at churches and other organizations, sharing his knowledge and expertise with others eager to learn. He has presented or served on panels at the University of North Carolina at Greensboro, Winston-Salem State University, Elon University School of Law, North Carolina Agricultural and Technical State University, the University of North Carolina School of Law at Chapel Hill, and Duke University.

Outside of his professional endeavors, Micah E. Huggins enjoys modeling and has appeared in commercials for national brands. His inspiring story of leadership, determination, and passion for life motivates and inspires countless others to reach for the stars and fulfill their full potential. He is a devoted husband and father of three.